The Boys
of Wasioja

By Michael Eckers

Photos on front cover
Top: Minnesota Historical Society
Bottom: Dodge County Historical Society

Illustrations by Jan Sease

Layout and Design by Heather Tollers

Published by Community News Corporation

Printed in the United States of America

FOREWARD

In 1990 I moved my family from San Diego, California to Owatonna, Minnesota. Shortly after the move a new friend invited me to visit the ruins of a seminary about 20 miles east in an area called Wasioja. While there I first heard the story of the students who had enlisted in the Union army from the school and of the demise of the town that resulted at their departure.

Over the years I continued to hear stories of Wasioja; it's founding and rapid growth, being named for a native chief who later saved the residents from the attack of another unidentified tribe. The stories are many and varied, each painting Wasioja in a unique landscape.

I have attempted, whenever possible, to focus the research for this book on original source documents. My appreciation goes to the Dodge County Historical Museum and the Minnesota State Historical Society for their assistance with this project.

It has always been my purpose to relate the truth about the outstanding men of Dodge County that served in Company C of the Second Minnesota Volunteer Infantry and their accomplishments. If Tom Brokaw had lived in the 1880's he certainly would have called these men "America's Greatest Generation."

12-20

Wasioja Seminary in 1860
Photo – Dodge County Historical Museum

TABLE OF CONTENTS

ACKNOWLEDGEMENT

This book would not have been possible without the courage, determination, and selflessness of those men who desired nothing more than the continuation of these United States. They answered the call of an idea whose embodiment in a country was at risk of fading away after only 80 years. To them we all owe a great debt.

I am also grateful for the limitless support of friends and family during the researching and writing of this work. To Diane, my wife of more than thirty years; to my children who have all added their own talents to this effort, my sincere thanks. To Jan, who has, once again, provided wonderful artwork in the maps she has created. Wayne, I honestly cannot imagine how long this would have taken without your help. My thanks to the Dodge County Historical Society, the Minnesota History Museum, and especially the Friends of Wasioja, all of whom gave me the help I asked for, and then some, along with encouragement that cannot be measured.

COMMANDERS
of the Second Minnesota Volunteer Infantry

Horatio Van Cleve
July 23, 1861–March 21, 1862

James George
May 15, 1862–June 29, 1864

Judson Bishop
March 5– July 11, 1865

Introduction
SEPTEMBER 1863

The men were working hard, with their grumbling as well as their hands. The undergrowth in these woods was so thick you couldn't see more than a few yards. They could hear the swelling noise of battle in front; it was the only way to tell that they were heading in the right direction. The further they struggled forward, the more wounded and frightened men would appear, heading the other direction. Several arms pointed ahead to the left; there were six men, with guns, carrying another in a blanket. Someone said it must be a general since the men were still armed and there were so many. At that moment a rebel shell came in, shrieking its deadly scream. As it exploded near them, the six men dropped their wrapped cargo and took off running through the Minnesota line to the rear. As quickly as they ran by, someone noticed the "wounded" man in the blanket jump up and run after them, actually passing them in his hurry to get away. About all the boys from Company C could do was stand and laugh; at least it provided some distraction from the deadly work ahead of them. As they cleared the woods and crossed the La Fayette road several men stopped and stared at the sight in front of them. Everywhere they looked was confusion, no organized lines of soldiers. Many were walking or running to the rear, but where was the rear? The noise of guns firing came at them from three directions; they could see the rising clouds of smoke from Confederate rifles ahead and to both sides as they advanced.

Suddenly Lt Colonel Bishop's horse went down, throwing the Colonel over its head to the ground. Getting up, Bishop ordered the men to form a line and begin firing at the rebels to their left along a line of trees. The enemy had the cover and the Second had to stand and receive a terrible fire as they blazed away in return. In a matter of minutes 70 or so Minnesotans were on the ground, dead and wounded, including several from Company C. It seemed as though you could reach up a hand and fill it with bullets, something you thought about but never tried. Colonel George, still very ill, was the only officer mounted and he began to give orders to lengthen the line. At that moment help arrived as the other regiments in the brigade came up on their right and left. It was good to see the 87th Indiana, 9th and 35th Ohio again. The brigade commander, Colonel Van Derveer, took charge and soon the yanks were pouring a good fire into the rebel lines. To the left of the Second, the 9th Ohio saw the rebels begin to break and charged into the woods after them. Company E of the Second followed in the charge; Colonel George then ordered the remainder of the Second in as well, breaking the lines of the 60th North Carolina. The rebel attack had been beaten back at that point and this small section of the immense battle was quieting down. It had been a lively half hour or so but all around them the sounds of battle were still heard and it seemed things were not going well for the yankees elsewhere. The day was not yet half over and everyone knew there was more fighting ahead.

Chapter 1
MAY 1861

The town had existed for only five years. In the spring of 1856 the first land was platted that was to become Wasioja. Curtis Moses and James George had a vision and the energy to see it through. It seemed to have literally shot up out of the ground. The first hotel, a log one, had gone up in May of 1857. Before it was even completed another, larger one was being built. The town was on the Zumbro River with the territorial stage road running through. Surrounded by fine farm land there was a limestone quarry on the banks of the river at the edge of the newly laid out town site. It was hoped that railroads could be enticed to come here and, perhaps, the county seat would be located in Wasioja as well.

In 1858 construction began on a school for higher learning which would be run by the Free Will Baptists; limestone from the local quarry was used in its construction. Despite a pause in its building because of the economic Panic of 1858 and a destructive hailstorm in July of that year, the school was completed and opened in November of 1860. In January 1862 the name was changed to Northwestern College and eventually enrolled as many as 200 students from "primary" through the "academic" level. Though there was talk

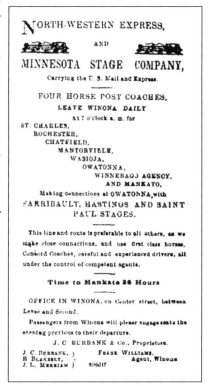

Winona Daily – July 1861

3

from back east about the possibility of war again with some of the southern states seceding from the Union, at a local level the future was indeed bright. The economy was improving, a new President had just taken office and Wasioja was growing again.

"I don't understand why you feel you need to go, Clinton. The school, with its mission to educate our young men, has a much greater need for you than this army being raised right now. There are more than enough other men to go fight the rebels and not nearly enough qualified professors." Reverend Williams, the principal was trying to control his own feelings. The new term had begun a few months ago and now his main professor was announcing a desire to leave, to go and fight in the newly declared war with the rebels. Certainly the young man could see the importance of remaining here at the school.

Boys of Wasioja
Company C
Second Minnesota

From those enrolled at the
Minnesota Seminary
January 1861

Faculty
Clinton A. Cilley
James George

Students
William M. Casseday
Freeman G. Castle
Harrison K. Couse
Edmund Garrison
Oscar P. Heath
Robert S. Hutchison
Samuel S. Kline
Theodore DeM. Orcutt
Darwin B. Rossiter
Benjamin F. Wood (1)

"Sir, I've been speaking with Mr George....actually Captain George now, about this very issue. He agrees with the need for schools but has convinced me of the importance of guaranteeing the very future of the school and the threat to it that this war brings. We need to put down this rebellion and, naturally it will require sacrifice to do so. If we all listened to the numerous reasons not to fight, the south would just drift away and the Union would be no more. I've quite decided to go, as have many of the students of the school itself. I'll be in a position to help to oversee them personally; the Captain has recommended me for the position of a leading Sergeant in the new company he's organizing. I've also been in contact with my father; he is already serving as a chaplain in a New Hampshire regiment and my brother is an officer as well."

Neither man could have imagined what the cost would be to the school before the war was over. Of the 53 boys enrolled in the upper divisions at present, 26 would eventually sign on to fight for the Union. Ten would be in Company C of the Second Regiment, along with two of the faculty; the remaining 16 would be in eight other units from the state. All would fight either the Confederates or the Dakota Indians.

As the professor and principal were conversing, nearly a dozen of the Northwestern students were gathered outside waiting for Professor Cilley to lead them over to Captain George's law office to begin the process of joining the army. The past couple of days had been filled with stirring speeches and bands playing music and general excitement as the Captain and others had worked at raising a company of volunteers to help suppress the southern rebellion. Many of the men of the area had formed a militia company back in early May and were spending their spare time drilling and learning to become soldiers.

Captain George had fought in the Mexican War before he became a founder of Wasioja and was one of the most respected men in the town. With the help of Peter Mantor from nearby Mantorville, he had been able to raise nearly 100 men in a short time, many from this town, but others from villages and townships here in Dodge County. They had not been quick enough to get into the first regiment to rep-

James George's Law Office
Photo – Author's Collection

resent the new state of Minnesota, but now a second regiment was being called up and the rush to become part of it was on.

The First Minnesota had been formed out of companies of state militia that already existed, units formed over the years to provide protection from possible Indian attacks. Though a state for three years now, Minnesota was still the edge of the frontier and Indian troubles were not unheard of. The First had been formed in just a couple of weeks following the southern attack on Fort Sumter in South Carolina that had begun the "fighting war." Governor

Alexander Ramsey happened to be in Washington DC when news of the attack reached the War Department. Ramsey immediately offered 1,000 troops to assist in putting down the Confederacy, making Minnesota the first state to offer troops. Now all ten companies of the First had been formed and the Governor was calling for another regiment of 1,000 to help fight and to relieve the regular U.S. troops that manned the three forts guarding the frontier. Fort Ridgely was on the Minnesota River near the Sioux Reservations, Fort Ripley was in the center of the state on the Mississippi River and Fort Abercrombie was in the northwest corner of Minnesota near the border with Canada.

What would eventually become Company C of the Second Minnesota was getting ready to head to Fort Snelling, near the capital in St Paul, to be mustered into the U S Army. Some of the group were already becoming known as the "Boys of Wasioja."

ATTENTION COMPANY!

The Dodge County Volunteers will meet at Mantorville on Saturday the 22nd inst., at 10 o'clock A.M. under orders received from Head Quarters to hold themselves in readiness to march without delay. Every member of the company, and all others desirous of becoming members are requested to be in attendance.
By order of
J. George,
Capt. commanding

H. K. Couse, O. S.
Mantorville June 15, 1861

Mantorville Express
of Friday, June 21st, 1861

Chapter 2
SUMMER 1861

Following several days of gatherings, speeches and dinners, the men from Dodge County loaded into wagons and left Mantorville on June 25th. That evening they were feasted in Pine Island and housed for the night. The next day found them heading for Wabasha on the Mississippi where they boarded a steamboat and headed upriver to Fort Snelling at the confluence of the Mississippi and Minnesota Rivers. Captain A. D. Nelson of the Regular Army mustered and swore them in on the 29th of June 1861. The 100 men that made up Company C were mostly from Dodge and Wabasha Counties with a sprinkling from elsewhere around the state. A few men from Dodge County traveled by themselves and arrived days later; as a result they were placed in other companies, most ending up in Company K. The origins of the companies were as follows:

Company A	Fillmore County
Company B	Olmsted County
Company C	Dodge County
Company D	Ramsey County
Company E	Nicollet County
Company F	Washington County
Company G	Ramsey and Brown Counties
Company H	Blue Earth County
Company I	Goodhue County
Company K	Recruited at large

Their training would begin very soon. Once they had been issued uniforms and some equipment, they were dispatched to the training forts: Abercrombie, Ripley and Ridgely.

Company A left for Fort Ripley on foot, a distance of 130 miles, on July 3rd.

They were followed a few days later by Company F. Companies B and C went to Fort Abercrombie and Companies D and E to Fort Ridgely; the other four companies remained at Fort Snelling. They were to remain at these posts for several weeks.

Later in July, on the 22nd, Governor Ramsey appointed

Winona Daily July 27, 1861

H.P. Van Cleve as Colonel of the regiment, along with Lieutenant Colonel George and Major Simeon Smith. Major Smith was shortly made a paymaster in the Regular Army and his place taken by Captain Alexander Wilkin of the First Minnesota. Other appointments included Reginald Bingham as Surgeon and Reverend Timothy Cressey as Chaplain. Colonel Van Cleve had been an officer in the Regular Army, George and Wilkins had fought as volunteer officers during the Mexican War in 1847. No other officer in the regiment had any known field experience. During their stay at Fort Abercrombie the Company C men endured bad water, bad food, scorching hot weather, mosquitoes and sickness. Shortly after their arrival Private Levi Sanborn of Ashland died of heat exhaustion (July 19, 1861). Sanborn was to be the first of many of Company C that would not return to Dodge County. A few short weeks later he would be joined by Private Julius Wheeler, also of Ashland, who fell victim to the heat and disease (August 5, 1861). Neither of them would rest long in the Dakota Territory; in the 1880's they were reburied in the Custer National Cemetery at

We have got some new clothes in the shape of uniform; overcoats, gray cloth – military dresscoats, blue cloth with brass buttons – blowses, blue woolen drill – gray woolen shirts, good woolen socks, and good shoes. No pantaloons yet – some of the boys need them badly. You all would hardly know the boys to see them on dress parade, they look and act like soldiers and gentlemen. Elder Morse is clerk in the Quartermaster's department and Grable is carpenter for post at extra pay. Young Sanborn died last night before we reached here, and was buried with the honors of war. Several of the boys have been and some still are sick, mostly with diarrhea – nothing dangerous I think. William Orcutt of Concord is in the hospital with a sore throat. Uncle Sam

Mantorville Express, August 9, 1861

the Little Bighorn Battlefield.

The two month stay at Fort Abercrombie would claim one more victim from the unofficial ranks of Company C. Captain Peter Mantor's wife had come along, as many officers' wives did during the War. She died in early September before the Company was ordered back to Fort Snelling to prepare for departure to the southern battlefields. Her death moved Captain Mantor to resign his commission on December 4, 1861; this resulted in the transfer and promotion of First Lieutenant Daniel Heaney from Company B to the captaincy of Company C.

Chapter 3

FALL 1861

The Second Regiment was fully assembled for the first time during early October. Nearly all the companies were full (maximum of 101 men per company). The regiment numbered more than 1,000 men including the regimental band and support staff.

The morning of October 14th the Second marched through the streets of St Paul to the lower levee to embark on a steamboat for the war. Few could see that of the 1,000 "muskets" and 36 "swords" that made up the parade, that less than 300 enlisted and only 3 officers would be returning with the flags they so proudly carried that day. The steamboat ride ended at La Crosse, Wisconsin where the men were put aboard the railroad and arrived in Chicago on the 16th. The men were quartered in the Wigwam, where Abraham Lincoln had won the Republican nomination a year earlier. The next day they boarded a train and arrived in Pittsburg, Pennsylvania on the 18th; their destination was to be Washington DC to join the First Minnesota in her brigade.

In Pittsburg, Colonel Van Cleve learned of a change in orders; the Second was to proceed to Kentucky to become part of the Department of the

Second Regiment at Fort Snelling—1861
Photo – Minnesota History Museum

Cumberland under the command of Brigadier General William T Sherman. After another riverboat ride they arrived in Louisville on the 22nd of October 1861. Colonel Van Cleve and Captain Judson Bishop of Company A reported the regiment as present to the General. *"When the Second Minnesota passed through on Monday, some two dozen of our first ladies, who were making up various articles of clothing for the soldiers, ran out of the house where they were working, waving the articles, and greeting the Minnesotans as they marched by. The Minnesota Regiment, in turn, waved their hats and gave three times three cheers for the ladies of Old Kentucky."* (1)

The Second was ordered to continue on to Lebanon Junction, about 30 miles south by railroad; they traveled all night through a cold rain aboard open flatcars for their reception into the front lines of the war. Timothy Pendergast, a soldier in Company K, recorded, *"Here we established our camp in a field, the railroad in our front, a heavy growth of beech timber in our rear, the road to Lebanon on our right flank, and the river a short distance away on our left. Here began our real duty as soldiers."* (2)

The unpleasant weather kept the Second boys pretty close to their quarters in the Wigwan yesterday. The provisions for the inner man were purchased in abundance by our citizens. The Tremont House undertook the job of supplying the men with a dinner at two hours' notice, and accomplished the work on time, and in a handsome manner. The order for the dinner – all hot – was given at 12 o'clock, and at 2:30 the following bill of fare was ready to be served to the hungry men: 1,000 pounds of war corned beef; 700 loaves of bread; 15 bushels of boiled potatoes, and 10 bushels of baked beans.

Chicago Tribune – October 16, 1861

Chapter 4
WINTER 1861–62

The Second was to become part of a brigade which included the 9th Ohio, 35th Ohio and 19th U S Regular Infantry. The brigade was commanded by Colonel R F McCook and was in a division commanded by Brigadier General George H Thomas. The men of Dodge County would rise to distinguished service under Thomas. They would remain at Lebanon Junction, excepting local actions, through to the summer of 1862. While there, sickness abounded as it did in all of the early Civil War army camps. Before their time at the Junction was completed, five more Dodge County men would die of sickness: Alexander Brown of Berne (November 24, 1861), Ferdinand Guild of Mantorville (January 6, 1862), Nathan Chase of Mantorville (January 8, 1862), Henry Hardin of Concord (February 21, 1862) and Charles Oline of Wasioja (February 22, 1862). All five now rest in National Cemeteries in Kentucky with the exception of Chase, whose gravesite is, at present, unknown.

At this time Lt Colonel Bishop records a humorous tale about soldiers and campfires: *"General Buell had issued an order that no private property should be appropriated by the troops without proper authority, and thus far the fuel had been provided by the quartermaster, but one evening we encamped in some open fields where there was no cut wood or forest accessible. The fields were, however, well fenced with dry rails and, after some exasperating delay, authority was obtained to use in this emergency "only the top rail" of the fence along the color line. The cheery camp fires were soon blazing, and we had plenty of fuel all the long night; next morning the fence was entirely gone. The company commanders were called to account for this disappearance but were unable to find any man who took any but the 'top rail.'"* (1)

The military situation in this part of Kentucky was muddled at best. Confederate General Felix Zollicoffer was in command of the rebel forces centered at an area known as Beech Grove near where Fishing Creek joins the Cumberland River. Union forces under General Schoepf were at Somerset, about seven miles east of Beech Grove. McCook's brigade, including the Second Minnesota had marched to Logan's Crossroads, nine miles north of rebel position. It became Zollicoffer's plan to defeat each Union position separately before they could join forces against him. The resulting battle became known as Mill Springs (it is also called Fishing Creek and Logan's Crossroads).

Colonel George wrote a letter to his children on January 13th which describes a bit of the confusion: *"Here we are in camp about 16 miles from the enemy who is on the Cumberland River at the mouth of White Oak Creek just above Jamestown, I think you can find it on the map. We know nothing yet of his force & position when we get up to him we will act according to circumstances, either fight or entrench & wait for reinforcements. Some say he will run; that he has not more*

Battle of Mill Springs
Original painting by Robert Cull – "Only a Fence Between Us"

than 9,000 men. Others say he has 25,000; so you see we must look at him & survey his position before we can determine anything." (2)

On the morning of January 19th the Confederates attacked McCook's brigade. The Second Minnesota was awakened by the drummers beating "the long roll" for the first time. The Fourth Kentucky and Tenth Indiana were in the front of the Union position and bore the brunt of the attack. After standing fast for more than a half hour both Union regiments began to run low on ammunition. The Second Minnesota and 9th Ohio were called upon to relieve them. At a fence the Second faced off against the Twentieth Tennessee which had also just arrived on the field. As Colonel McCook noted in his official report, *the contest was at first almost hand-to-hand; the enemy and the Second Minnesota were poking their guns through the same fence."* News was passed down the line that General Zollicoffer had been killed in the fighting. The Union troops took advantage of this by launching a bayonet charge that broke the rebel lines and forced them from the field in a rout.

A few days later the following letter, written by a member of the Second Minnesota was printed in the New York Times, having been first printed in the Detroit Tribune:

"Shortly after the Tenth Indiana was relieved by the appearance of the Fourth Kentucky, the two Tennessee regiments also came up. This force is composed of the most bloodthirsty men we have got, for the majority of them have been driven from their homes by the Secessionists. The four regiments named stood the brunt of the fight, the Second Minnesota and the Ninth Ohio having been kept back as a reserve, and the Tenth and Twelfth Kentucky and the Fourteenth Ohio did not arrive until just as the enemy started on the retreat, as they were encamped some seven miles in back of us. When the battle had raged near two hours, the Tenth Indiana and the Fourth Kentucky were withdrawn, and the Second Minnesota and the Ninth Ohio were ordered in.

Our regiment formed in line and Colonel Van Cleve, as brave a man as ever lived, rushed to the front with drawn sword and revolver, and gave the command "Forward, double quick, march" when our men rushed to the front with an Indian war-whoop that struck fear to the heart of every secesher, going up to within fifteen feet of the enemy, when they halted and poured a most terrific volley right into the faces of the rebels. This was considered the most terrible and effective volley delivered during the entire engagement. Our boys stood their ground like heroes, never flinching an inch, our gallant Colonel riding up and down the lines through a perfect hailstorm of bullets, cheering on our men continually, and our prisoners state that the 'Minnesota Indian boys' as they called them did more damage than any other regiment.

Not one of our regiment officers was wounded or hurt, but we had eleven brave fellows killed, and as many more wounded, one or two of whom will, perhaps, die."

The letter was written by a soldier who signed it "Jim." Company C was involved in the fighting and records show that two men in it were wounded though none were killed. Neither of the wounded was from Dodge County.

Following the fighting, the Federals pursued the rebels several miles to where the Confederate fortifications stood overlooking the river on the north bank. As darkness spread, General Thomas called a halt to the advance to have a better look at the entrenched enemy. By morning northern artillery had thrown some shells into the southern position; when no response was noted, an advance party was ordered forward to scout ahead. They found the rebel camp deserted and a tremendous amount of food and supplies left behind, along with more than a thousand horses and mules. The Second Minnesota marched into the former camp of the Twentieth Tennessee and discovered a treasure trove of bedding, food, and clothing inside the tents. Claiming it as their own, they camped there

Silk flag presented by Ladies of Louisville
Photo – Minnesota Historical Society

until they returned to their own camp at Logan's Crossroads on the 21st and marched to Somerset, Kentucky on the 23rd where they camped two miles south of the town.

During the fight, the Minnesota men captured the colors of the Fifteenth Mississippi which were forwarded on to the War Department in Washington. They were also rewarded with a beautiful silk flag commemorating the victory by the Loyal Ladies of Louisville, which resides today in the state capitol in St Paul. The presentation of this flag was made in late February as General Thomas's division returned to Louisville.

As the men of the Second Minnesota were marching through Kentucky,

15

General Grant, with much help from the Navy, had defeated Confederate forces at Forts Henry and Donelson. This caused the rebels to withdraw their armies from Tennessee and relocate to Corinth, Mississippi. Toward the end of March, General Grant concentrated his forces for another push south at a town in southern Tennessee called Pittsburg Landing where a small church, named Shiloh, is located.

Chapter 5

SPRING 1862

Most of February and March were spent by the Second Minnesota in marching through Kentucky and Tennessee with the rest of General Buell's army. Their purpose was to further drive rebels south and to consolidate the Union's hold on the two states. The regiment arrived in Nashville on March 3rd and camped on the Granny Smith Road for about three weeks. The men received much needed rest and were resupplied with new uniforms and equipment. Many of the sick and injured men that had been left behind in Kentucky now rejoined the regiment. In mid March General Buell was ordered to join General Halleck's forces on the Tennessee River near the town of Savannah, a few miles upriver from Pittsburg Landing. They were to join General Grant in his push to Corinth. General Thomas's division was placed last in the line of march because they had already participated in a major battle (Mill Springs).

The Battle of Shiloh (April 6 & 7th) has had much written about it. Confederate forces under the command of Generals AS Johnston and PG Beauregard surprised Union troops commanded by Generals WT Sherman and US Grant. The fighting was unlike anything up to this point in the War. On the first day the rebel army forced the Union toward the banks of the Tennessee River, nearly destroying it. General Grant, however, reorganized during the night and on the second day launched a vicious attack that pushed the Confederates back several miles and caused them to retreat to their base in Corinth. General Albert Sidney Johnston, considered by some to be the best of the Confederate leaders, was killed late in the first day's fight. Before the Battle of Shiloh casualties were considered extreme if they had reached 500 on each side. In the two days fighting at Pittsburg Landing, the number of killed, wounded or missing/captured totaled over 13,000 for the north and nearly 11,000 for the south. This civil war would never be the same; Shiloh marked the beginning of the huge battles that became the trademark of the war.

The Second Minnesota did not take part in the Battle of Shiloh. Marching at the tail end of General Buell's army, they arrived on the battlefield the day after the fighting ended. Major Bishop recorded the task facing the new arrivals: *"...so we had to perform the burial of about 4,000 men, gathering them from every part of the battlefield. Some lay where they had first fallen; others lived long enough to crawl to some nearby thicket or gully for protection or for water. Some lay in attitudes of rest, their faces showing nothing of suffering or fear; others had evidently died in great agony. Some were identified by comrades, and of such the graves were rudely marked, but many of our dead and nearly all the Confederates were unknown and unrecognized. They were laid side by side in long shallow pits and were covered, a hundred or more, in one grave. Many of the wounded had been able to find their own way to the field hospitals, but several thousand of them were taken up on the field and carried off on stretchers or in ambulances. Some of these were not found until two or three days after the battle. All of this was very sad business; none who participated in it or witnessed it will ever forget it. Men can, in the enthusiasm and excitement of battle, see and take part in the murderous work without realizing how horrible it is, but to go over the field the day afterwards, and in cool blood, to gather up the mangled and suffering victims, gives one a life-long impression of the cruelty of war and of its pitiful waste of human life."* [1]

It was three days later that the regiment first moved from the Shiloh Battlefield. William Bircher, a regimental drummer boy from Company K, kept a detailed diary during the Second's service time. He wrote: *"Then we marched four miles south to a camp called Gravelly Hill. Here we were supplied with water from a spring strongly impregnated with iron, and the boys had a very strong idea that they were improving in health wonderfully while they were using it."* (2)

During this period the health of the men from Dodge County continued to improve slightly, or it could have been that those who would be the sickest had already died. Colonel George's wife wrote a letter to her daughter, Helen, and mentions several of the local "boys":

"April 15th, 1862

(Benjamin) Frank Wood took dinner with us today he is better. Edmond Garrison is well he went last night to help (Morgan) Lou Wood to the Hospital and stayed all night with him without leave. When he came back this morning they put him in the guard house Pa found it out and let him out in a hurry. (Harrison) Couse does well but there is no prospect of his being promoted. Helen he is a good boy don't dislike him he too has a hard time of it. Darwin (Rossiter) came out from the Hospital tonight feeling well he was not much sick. I think Theodore (Orcutt) is quite sick yet but is on the mend so Elder Cressey told Pa tonight. I know the Casseday (John & William) boys I think they are not sick; I will try and find out and tell you before we send this." (3) It is fair to note that Harrison Couse was, in fact, promoted later that year. Darwin Rossiter actually received a disability discharge on May 16th, 1862. In addition, disability discharges were granted to Samuel Burwell (5/13), Edward Orcutt (5/18) and Benjamin [Frank] Wood (5/18). These were to be the last given in the company for several months.

It was during this period of relative inactivity (except for the daily entrenching), that another letter was written giving good descriptions of those who were serving so far from Dodge County. Clinton Cilley, former professor from the Seminary, wrote this to Helen George, the Colonel's daughter on May 14th.

"The Wasioja boys deserve a detailed account. To begin with the tallest: Lee. He joined us soon after we got over this side of the river and behaved very quietly and well until one Sunday, moving with the wagons, as wagon guard, he got beastly drunk, fell to quarreling and gambling and lost two-

thirds of his four months pay. Since then he has been stiller and more sub-
dued than ever. His health is good. He is a good soldier when sober, albeit,
maybe, a bit excitable in danger.

HK Couse is first sergeant and makes a good one. He tents and messes
with the second lieutenant and myself. The Cassedays, William and John,
are as good boys and as good soldiers as ever were in a company. Mrs
Casseday ought to be proud of having three such men as her husband and
two sons in the service. They are strong, tough and well.

Rossiter's discharge has been made out and forwarded to division and
department headquarters. We expect it every day. His spirit is good, but he
is not tough enough to endure the terrible life we have led. This regiment, I
believe, has had the hardest service of any in the pay of the government.

Tooke is our cook and is one of the best men, every way, in the regiment. I
have a very great regard for him. He manages our company rations so they
go as far as possible and saves a great deal in company fund. Corporal
Wood behaves nicely, does his duty faithfully and endures hardship. He
stays with me a good share of the time. He is well.

Little Rob Hutchison is a corporal now. He is a grand, good fellow and sol-
dier. He, Bonser, Capon and I are the only ones in the company who have
never been off duty for sickness. He is in good health, of course.

Ben Wood is at McBeoler's yet, so far as I know. His discharge papers have
been forwarded twice, but he has never received them. Ed Garrison is just
the same as ever, cool, strong and good. Dick Shedd is very much the same
as in Wasioja, save that he grows careless of his personal habits and doesn't
look as clean and tidy as he might. Alex Doig is a good man, given a little to
complaining and murmuring, but does his duty and keeps well.

Some say that Theodore Orcutt is at home again. I hope so – his health will
not allow him to serve and a sick man is never so much out of place as in the
army.

Cartwright is back in hospital again; his constitution seems broken down.
Russ does very well nowadays is quite well and carries his regular load
without grumbling. Corporal Townsend has improved of late and is a very
good soldier and tough man, though he is a little troubled with a rheumatic
arm.

Dick is improving, too, and since he failed to get a discharge is getting well
very fast – he never will make a soldier, though. The celebrated Kline is – the

Lord knows where! The last I heard of him he was a hospital nurse at Lebanon. He is not sick at all himself.

There is a row out ahead here, somewhere, I guess, as several regiments have just gone along with fixed bayonets. I've heard no firing, but there may be something on foot. At any rate I'll stop and write again shortly. With much regard, I am,

Your Sincere Friend,

Clinton A. Cilley" (4)

Colonel George also spoke of the improving health of the regiment in a letter to his wife and family in mid May:

"In Camp May 16, 1862

Dear Wife & Children, Well we were out again yesterday driving in the rebels. We had an awful hot march but no body hurt. The weather here is intensely hot. I believe it has not hurt me so far. I have secured additional medical aid since I got command & the health of my men is steadily improving. We are now about four miles from Corinth & 3 from the enemy's ranks. No one knows when an attack will be made. The forces on either side are immense. The 4th Regiment is about 8 miles East of us have not seen any of them yet. (Clinton) Cilley says he wrote to you yesterday; he now commands Co C. (Daniel) Heany has gone on staff duty with General Van Cleve. I have now 600 men for duty." (5)

Following the Battle of Shiloh, General Halleck took command of the western army. General Grant was second in command, General Sherman became the division commander and Colonel Van Cleve was promoted to Brigadier General and given command of a brigade. Lt Colonel George was also promoted to Colonel and put in command of the Second Minnesota. Major Bishop advanced to Lt Colonel and Clinton Cilley became a First Lieutenant in Company C. During this time of reorganization the Federal troops were moving, at a snail's pace, toward the enemy at Corinth. General Halleck was intent on not repeating any form of surprise as had happened at Pittsburg Landing. The army moved about a half mile each day and fully entrenched at day's end. It took more than a full month to cover the distance from the Shiloh battlefield to the outskirts of Corinth, about 22 miles as the crow flies.

As the northern army crept ever closer to Corinth, a soldier from Company E (Nicollet County) had just rejoined the regiment after spending a short time recruiting back up in Minnesota. Bernt Olmanson wrote a letter home on May 25th:

" *We are now three miles from Corinth, Mississippi. Everything has been quiet the last two days. Ever since Al came back to the regiment there has been much uneasiness, small skirmishes every day. Many have been wounded, a few killed. But none of our regiment have been killed or wounded, although the shots and shells have been screaming around us while we were on picket duty.*

Three companies from each regiment are on picket duty all the time. Our battle line is about 15 miles long in a semi-circle around the Rebels. There is an entrenchment of timber and dirt along the whole line. The Rebel entrenchment is two miles away. Between us is a small stream which both sides are holding on to, as there is a shortage of water, especially before the rain on Thursday and Friday.

We have plenty of crackers, pork and coffee. Soft bread can sometimes be bought for 15-20 cents for an ordinary 5 cent loaf. Eggs are 30-40 cents a dozen. Butter is 40-50 cents a pound. Whiskey is $6-8 a gallon. Newspapers 10 cents each." [6]

The victory Halleck was slowly preparing for finally eluded him. On May 30th the Confederates slipped away from Corinth. The next day the Federal troops discovered their absence. What they left behind was, in the main, a foul and fetid camp that had little clean water sources and the Union commanders were forced to spread out their own divisions to avoid the overcrowded conditions the rebels had been living in.

Chapter 6
SUMMER 1862

As spring gave way to summer, the weather grew hotter and seemed to fluctuate from very dry to very humid. Again there was a reorganization of the army which seemed to please the Regiment as it ended up with General George Thomas commanding their division once again. July 1st found the Second in Tuscumbia, Alabama near a huge spring of cold, clear water. There they celebrated Independence Day with cannon salutes and speeches by generals and a visit by Governor Ramsey.

At the end of their first year of service, the Second Minnesota found itself far from home. The men had endured long marches through rain and dust, had slept without tents or blankets during miserable weather, had gone through periods of little or no food and had suffered for all of it. Company C had lost a total of 14 enlisted men and, through death or transfer, 5 officers. In the Civil War, a company had only 3 officers assigned; Captain, 1st and 2nd Lieutenants. Had it not been for the closeness of the men themselves there would have been more of a breakdown as a unit with this lack of consistent leadership. No one had died as a result of combat; the company had been spared serious casualties at Mill Springs. Sickness had claimed most; promotion, a couple of the officers. Those that were left were hard, seasoned veterans.

Later in July, an incident that was little reported, combined with one that attracted much attention, resulted in a brief volcanic "letting off of steam" that demonstrated the edge people were living on at the time. Lt Colonel Bishop wrote of July 27th:

"...being Sunday, the usual inspection of troops was had, and this over, a good many officers and enlisted men of the several regiments availed themselves of the opportunity to attend divine service. The Presbyterian Church

was well filled, the usual congregation of resident women and children occu-
pying perhaps one third of the seats. The uniformed visitors were courte-
ously received and ushered in, mingling with the regular attendants wher-
ever there might be room. The opening services were of the usual character,
and the singing was heartily joined by the soldiers; the scripture readings
were attentively listened to, and all heads were reverently bowed when the
venerable minister said, 'Let us pray.' The prayer, we were afterwards told,
was the formal one prescribed by the Presbyterian church authority of the
South and contained an invocation of the divine blessing upon the "President
of the Confederate States and upon all the authority under him," and upon
the armies of the Confederate States, and a direct and earnest appeal that
confusion and defeat might overwhelm their enemies, who had invaded their
soil and threatened their institutions and their liberties. This had not been
generally expected by the visitors, and it produced at the instant quite an
appreciable commotion. A variety of ejaculations, not in the usual line of
liturgical responses, were heard in various parts of the house, and some got
up and walked out to vent their indignation in the open air.

Most of us remained, however, to see the services through. The prayer
ended, the sermon began – a simple, earnest, well-composed and well-deliv-
ered discourse, interesting, edifying and in every way exceptional. The
preacher was himself the personification of Christian grace and dignity in
the pulpit, and we were soon in the mood to ignore, if we could not forgive
or forget, the offensive prayer. He had probably half completed his discourse
when the tramp of marching men was heard coming down the main aisle,
and a squad of the provost guard "halted" and "fronted" at the altar before
the minister. A colonel of infantry led the detachment, and now he inter-
rupted the preacher, charged him with insulting the uniform of the United
States and those who wore it, in addressing a disloyal petition to the
Almighty in their presence, and commanded him to come down and surren-
der to arrest. The minister gracefully bowed in compliance and, closing his
sermon book, came down and said he was "at your service, sir." Now the
ladies interposed, some with tears and pleadings, and some with sneers and
taunts at the imposing show of armed men in a peaceful church where only
women and children were present to protest, and some fainted, while the
colonel marched his guard and prisoner out and to headquarters. The
women then appealed to those of us who remained. They were assured that

their pastor was not led out to be shot and that probably no physical harm would be done to him. As soon as we could without rudeness, we withdrew to discuss in our camp the experiences and events of the morning. The prisoner was sent north under arrest, but what charges were formally preferred, or what, if any, trial or punishment he may have had, was never known to us." [1]

Two days later the Minnesota troops marched 9 miles through choking dust, followed by daily marches of 16, 16 and 14 miles. The men were hot, dirty, thirsty and tired; in short, not in the mood to be trifled with. The next day, brigade commander General McCook was ambushed by Confederate cavalry as he traveled, sick, in an ambulance. Unable to even lift himself from his bed, he was shot in cold blood. He died the next day; his brigade, especially his former regiment from Ohio, went a little crazy. William Bircher picks up the story:

"As a revenge the brigade burnt every house within a radius of two miles on each side of the road and slaughtered all the stock to be found. I heard that several suspicious looking characters had given up their lives also. From here we marched to the small village of Dorchester, Tennessee. From there to Winchester and through the town to Decherd Station, where we remained three days. Then we moved camp about one mile farther east, where we found a spring of sparkling, ice cold water." [2] One gets the feeling that the ice cold water was more notable than the revenge exacted for General McCook's demise.

While the Second Minnesota was marching and having a small personal war with the rebels, the Third Minnesota had been surrendered at Murfreesboro, Tennessee under extremely shameful circumstances. Under the command of Colonel Henry Lester the Third was part of a garrison which included several companies of a Michigan regiment and assorted small cavalry and artillery units, totaling some 1200 men. On July 13, 1862 a relatively unknown (at that time) Confederate cavalry commander named Nathan Bedford Forrest launched a surprise raid.

Capturing the Michigan commander, Forrest sent a letter to Colonel Lester stating *"I must demand an unconditional surrender of your forces as prisoners of war, or I will have every man put to the sword. You are aware of the overpowering force I have at my command, and this demand is made to prevent the further effusion of blood."* [3]

Lester fell for the bluff and, after consulting and voting with his junior officers, surrendered the entire regiment. Certainly not all, actually just a few, of the other officers favored surrender. The men of the Third were astonished that they had been given up without a fight. C C Andrews, a Captain who later became the Third's commander and a Brigadier General, noted that the Confederates were also amazed *"at the capture they had so cheaply made."* (4) The Minnesota officers were taken to Libby Prison in Richmond for a time before being exchanged; the enlisted men were to be sent to Jefferson Barracks in St Louis to remain until properly paroled. As it turned out, they were soon to be back in Minnesota fighting the Dakota after the Uprising of 1862 began a month or so later. The only troops to avoid this were those of Company C of the Third; that is how they became attached to the Second Minnesota for a period of time.

During the late summer into the fall the regiment spent days marching across Tennessee and Kentucky chasing various rebel cavalry and infantry raiders. At times their shoes completely wore out and the men were reduced to tying rags or pieces of uniforms around their feet in an attempt to protect them. By September they were exhausted. On September 3rd they were halted near Murfreesboro and camped next to a large field of watermelons; there are numerous reports in personal diaries and journals of the vast number of melons consumed by the men that evening. There is no mention, however, of the effect on their bowels for the next few days.

Chapter 7
FALL 1862

The only serious fighting that took place throughout all this marching (101 miles in August and 238 in September) was a skirmish over an apple orchard on September 19, near Cave City, Kentucky. As Colonel Bishop describes it: *"We found in our immediate front a big apple orchard, the trees all loaded with juicy fruit. The enemy's picket line was along the fence, on the further side, and their camps not far beyond. Our picket line was established along the fence on our side of the orchard, which was perhaps eighty rods across. Our men began to get over the fence and gather the apples, and the enemy's pickets fired at them. Our pickets in turn would not let the thirsty rebels get any apples out of their side of the orchard. The situation rapidly became known in the camps; and our picket line was in a few minutes reinforced by several hundred of the boys, who "straggled" out there with their guns, and presently our line was advanced with a rush to the further side of the orchard. The enemy's pickets resisted actively but retired just before our line reached them. They made an effort to regain their fence, but our boys wouldn't give it up. The advance troops in both armies got under arms upon hearing the racket, but the affair was probably reported to the generals as a "picket skirmish" of no consequence, and all became quiet that night. Several of the men were wounded, but none killed, in the skirmish, which was entirely an affair of the enlisted men. It looked at one time, however, as though a general fight might grow out of it right there and then, and we were all more than willing to have it so."* (1)

In early October the Battle of Perryville, Kentucky took place. Though the Second Minnesota was present, it was only as spectators. In one of nature's strange ways, the battle could not be heard by most of the commanders just a few miles away and the battle was fought only by a small part of the Union forces. Official reports put the toll at 916 killed, 2943 wounded and 484 missing for the north and more than 1300 killed for the south. The year 1862 ended with the regiment camped eleven miles outside Nashville, Tennessee. Though they could hear plenty of artillery fire from the Battle of Stone's River (December 31, 1862 through January 2, 1863) the men were not involved. Perhaps of greater importance to them, on an individual level, was a comparison of their senior officers. Throughout 1862 Colonel George had been absent for extended periods due to health and Lt Colonel Bishop would lead the regiment in his stead. Bernt Olmanson, of Company E, wrote home about their differences: *"Colonel George is well liked among the soldiers, but Lt Colonel Bishop is more particular. Bishop was away one month, then we did not have anything to do except when we marched. We did not even have to keep our camp nice. But since Bishop came back, we have to drill three hours a day."* (2)

Chapter 8
WINTER/SPRING 1863

As the new year began, some of the monotony that is soldiering started to settle on the men. On average, a civil war soldier faced 5 to 6 days of fighting each year. The other 360 were spent marching, drilling, building entrenchments and such. Bernt Olmanson, a soldier of Company E, wrote home about it on January 11th, *"It is said that we shall soon be ordered to the front. That is what we want because we have too much guard duty to do. I have been on guard duty three of the last five nights."* (1)

The faithful drummer boy of the Second, William Bircher, recorded that during 1862 the regiment had marched a total of 1493 miles while also experiencing other means of transport such as river boats, railroads and wagons. He was to keep a journal including the daily marches throughout the war. His journal is full of other interesting tidbits on the life of the regiment. Late in January he records a near disaster: *"While sitting in the tent, Christian Kersamair, of my company (K), had been using a twelve-pound elongated shell for an anvil to do some repairing on his knapsack, and, after getting through with it, he gave it a gentle kick and rolled it out of the tent. It rolled down into the fire in front of the tent, and in a few moments an explosion occurred that awoke the whole camp. It scattered the fire in such a shape that it was impossible to find a coal or a stick of the wood that had been there, and, most wonderful to say, no one was hurt. Our tent was covered an inch thick with ashes and dirt, and pieces of the shell flew all over the camp."* (2)

Though the Second marched plenty of miles chasing Confederate cavalry during the early part of the year, the only real action any saw happened when the enemy found them. In mid-February an exciting skirmish involved men of the regiment, though none of Company C were involved. As Lt Colonel Bishop recorded, *"a foraging party of two corporals and twelve men, under First Sergeant L.N. Holmes, all of Company H, went out to the front three or four miles for corn. They were loading their wagons from a large and well-filled crib when they were suddenly surrounded by two companies of Confederate cavalry, numbering about 125 men. The cavalry charged down upon them firing their carbines and yelling, "Surrender you d---d yanks."*

"Our boys in the crib did not think it necessary to surrender but commenced firing in return with deliberate aim, emptying a saddle with almost every shot, and the astonished cavalry soon quit yelling and withdrew out of range for consultation, then decided that they had had enough of the 'd---d yanks' and disappeared altogether. Our boys filled their wagons, picked up three of the wounded rebels and seven riderless horses which the enemy had left in the field, and returned safely to camp. Two of the wounded died the next day. Several others, slightly wounded, got away by the help of their companions. Colonel Van Derveer, commanding the brigade, was much elated by the brave conduct of the Second Minnesota boys and issued a special order complimenting them by name." (3) It should be noted that a total of eight Medals of Honor were later issued to the members of Company H who had been involved in this action.

The weather was very wet and the marching was mostly through mud. When the men had lived through a similar spring a year earlier, sickness had claimed many victims; this year everyone seemed to take it in stride and none of the Company C men were dangerously sick. Spring of 1863 brought much of the same; little action, lots of marching and wet weather. In early June an incident occurred that endeared Colonel George forever to the men of Company C, indeed all of the regiment. Bishop picks up the story: *"The day had been excessively hot and sultry, but now the sky grew black, and, after a severe thunderstorm, it settled down for a steady, heavy, all-night rain. That night's march (15 miles) will never be forgotten by the men of Van Derveer's brigade. The darkness was intense, the road soft, slippery and so uneven that some of the men were down or falling all the time. We were ten hours in making the march, arriving before daybreak utterly exhausted, and physically and mentally exasperated. The garrison seemed to be all asleep. No enemy was in the neighborhood, and we lay down in a lawn in the village to wait for dawn. Our field officers stretched themselves on the floor of the front porch of the spacious mansion. A little before sunrise, the front* door opened and a staff officer came out and, waking Colonel George with his foot, told him that the presence of the regiment on the premises was not agreeable to the lady owner and requested him to move on and out. The colonel had a talent for vigorous and emphatic profanity upon occasion, and he did his best there, but, as he afterwards acknowledged, no man could do justice to such hospitality as that. The officer who had aroused him slunk back into the house, withered and abashed, and did not appear again during the forenoon. In the afternoon, we made a reconnaissance in search of the enemy but found none." (4)

Chapter 9
CHICKAMAUGA

Later in June the brigade was on the move again, this time heading south toward the Tennessee with the intention of crossing it and forcing the Confederates out of Chattanooga. The river was wide and all the bridges had been burned by the retreating rebels. While the corps engineers got to work building new bridges for the wagons and artillery to cross, men of Company F (Lake St Croix lumber region) had been busy building rafts and scows for the Second to cross the river in. They made enough to allow four companies of the regiment to cross at once.

While the construction was going on, quite a lot of friendly banter was crossing the river between the soldiers of the two armies. First it consisted of bullets, but settled down into men swimming out to a small island in the middle of the river and trading newspapers, tobacco for coffee and other such items. The rebels became so accustomed to the yanks coming over that when the actual crossing was made, it was a total surprise. By the next day the entire brigade was over and the confederates were forced to continue their withdrawal southward.

The rest of the summer was spent by both armies maneuvering around southern Tennessee and northern Georgia in the vicinity of Chattanooga. All this movement was heading toward a major engagement along a sluggish creek whose name was a Cherokee name for "River of Blood" – Chickamauga. This book is not intended to be a military study of battles fought; for that there have already been countless fine works written by other authors. But an appropriate overview of the Second Minnesota's involvement in this critical and crucial fight is necessary.

The Battle of Chickamauga was fought over a period lasting two days. The fighting that took place ranks as some of the most terrible in history. The total casualties (killed, wounded, missing) for both armies totaled nearly 35,000. Hundreds more would die later of their wounds or from captivity. One man from Company C would die there, nine would be wounded, several quite badly.

The fighting at Chickamauga began shortly after first light on September 19th. General Thomas' corps was on the left of the Federal line running for miles on the west side of the creek. A strong Confederate force of dismounted cavalry was sent to swing around Thomas' left flank, using the thick underbrush to hide their movement.

General Brannan had ordered Van Derveer's brigade to advance down the Reed's Bridge road to try and flank the Confederates. The soldiers of the brigade were cooking breakfast when the order came. In disgust and frustration they gulped down their steaming hot coffee and formed up. Captain Jeremiah Donahower of Company E had already finished his coffee and was opening a can of pineapple when the orders came. He recalled that, swearing profusely they grabbed their cups *"and drank their coffee seasoned with the dust of the road as they marched. The cursing was too much for the Second's chaplain. 'Dreadful, dreadful,' he moaned as he listened. 'But think,' laughed a nearby soldier, 'how dreadfuller it would be*

Detail of monument at Reed's Bridge Road
Photo – Author's Collection

to go into battle and get killed with all those curses in 'em.'

General Brannan spoke to the Minnesotans as they passed by. In his own way he was saying to them that there were Rebels ahead and desperate work as well. As they marched the General greeted them with 'Now Minnesotans, step out.'" (1)

Minutes after the brigade arrived and formed up the rebels struck, totally surprised by the presence of union troops. This was the first of four separate attacks the Second would face in the next several hours, all of them from different directions and in an area of thick woods measuring only fifty square acres.

The fighting was of the worst type; the smoke quickly hiding what little was visible in the underbrush. The noise of thousands of rifles and dozens of cannon would cause many to go deaf, some permanently. The day was hot, with little or no breeze; canteens were emptied early, washing down the powder on the lips from biting open so many cartridges to load the muskets.

After the third attack, the Ninth Ohio came up to provide some additional manpower; this regiment had been guarding the corps ammunition wagons and their commander, Colonel Kammerling had spent much of the morning searching for someone who would order them into battle. The Ninth was made up entirely of Germans; orders were given in German and they fought using European tactics. As they came up, Van Derveer's men had just repulsed a rebel brigade from Mississippi. Colonel Kammerling shouted "Vere dem got tam rebels gone;" someone pointed to the front. The Ninth went after them on the run, shouting in German and all trying to be the first to get at the Confederates. It was only a short time later that they came back, also on the run, having lost a large number of their own when they hit the rebel line.

The last attack began when Captain Donahower of the Second spotted more rebels trying to outflank their position. Donahower informed Major Davis who found Lt Colonel Bishop. On this day, Colonel George was still greatly bothered by his rheumatism (he had only returned to the regiment two days earlier). Lt Colonel Bishop immediately ordered the Second to 'change front' to the east and file to the left across the road. Van Derveer ordered the rest of the brigade to follow the Minnesotans. By only minutes, again, the brigade had formed up to withstand another attack. Though they had lost around 250 men so far that morning, the addition of the 82nd Indiana regiment brought the brigade up to nearly 1800 men along with eight cannon to face a much

34

smaller force of the rebels. The attack lasted only a few minutes and cost the Confederates dearly. When it was over, Van Derveer's men marched back up the Reed's Bridge road to refill their cartridge boxes.

As busy as they had been, it was only the first of three separate engagements the Dodge County men would face in the two-day battle.

The next engagement for the Minnesotans was before mid-day on the 20th at a location known as Kelly Field. General Thomas' corps still held the left of the entire Union position. In order for General Rosecrans to successfully guard the possible retreat routes back to Chattanooga, it was imperative that Thomas hold his position, securing the Lafayette road and others. The morning of the second day of fighting found the Federal troops in good positions and in acceptable strength.

Monument at Kelly's Field
Photo – Author's Collection

Shortly after 9:00 a.m. the Confederates launched an attack against Thomas on the left. After an hour or so of fierce fighting, Thomas requested help. Rosecrans began shifting troops that way in anticipation of increased rebel pressure. In this, he violated one of those "rules" of war; do not move troops around a battlefield unless absolutely necessary, especially when your enemy is about to attack. As a result, the worst possible thing happened; while ordering troops out of positions in the center of his line to reinforce Thomas, Rosecrans unknowingly created a gap some 100 yards or so wide in the middle of his army. At the same moment, by chance, Confederate General James Longstreet launched the main rebel drive right at the vacant area. In what seemed like minutes, everything began to collapse.

It was 10:30 a.m. when Colonel Van Derveer's brigade, including the

Second Minnesota was ordered to march up across the Lafayette road to help out on the left flank. The Introduction to this book describes what happened next.

When the rebels were finally driven from Kelly Field the left of Rosecrans line was stable, but not for long. As the right and center of the Federal position gave way, Thomas was given the task of holding back the Confederates long enough for the rest of the Union army to retreat to Chattanooga. Once again, the Second Minnesota was called upon to move and form a battle line to help hold back the southern tide. The place is called Horseshoe Ridge; they would be helping defend the Snodgrass farm.

"The situation was growing a bit brighter for the Federals. Sometime between 2:30 and 3:00 p.m., Colonel Van Derveer rode into the Snodgrass cornfield at the head of his brigade. (General) Thomas rode out to meet the column. He told Van Derveer to take his men to Hills Two and Three and there relieve Brannan's tired troops. Thomas paused a moment to greet the Second Minnesota, which had made a timely charge to win the Battle of Mill Springs for him nearly two years before. 'Colonel, I want you to hold the hill,' he told the rheumatic James George. 'We will,

Monument at Snodgrass Hill
Photo – Author's Collection

36

general, until we are ordered away or are mustered out of service,' replied George. To Lieutenant Colonel Bishop, the de facto commander of the Second, Thomas spoke a few words of encouragement and complimented him on the 'good order' of his men.'" (2)

A forward position on the ridge was manned by the 21st Ohio equipped with five-shot Colt revolving rifles. The 21st had 535 men at the beginning of the fight that day; by now they had fired more than 45,000 rounds, driving back the Confederates several times as they tried moving up the ridge. The Ohioans had finally run out of ammunition and the men withdrew individually as they fired their last round, reforming behind the Second Minnesota on the reverse of the ridge. But the rebels were not through...

The men of the Second had about 10 rounds each as they waited for the rebel charge. *"Don't waste any cartridges now, boys,"* shouted Bishop. *"The men in gray commenced falling, but they seemed to bow their heads to the storm of bullets, and picking their way among and over their fallen comrades who already encumbered the slope by hundreds, they came bravely and steadily on. As, however, they approached nearer, and they seemed to lose the assuring touch of elbows, and as the vacancies rapidly increased, they began to hesitate – 'Now we've got 'em, see 'em wobble,' were the first words passed in our line since the firing had begun – then they halted and commenced firing wildly into the treetops, then turned and rushed madly down the slope."* (3)

Elsewhere along the Union line stretching in a semicircle along the high ground, other regiments were completely out of ammunition; some were arming themselves with rocks as the Confederates approached. Union General Granger arrived at that moment with the only reserve troops between Thomas and Chattanooga. A short time later the sun went down and the fighting stopped; it had been a very close affair.

Captain H. Dillard of the Sixteenth Tennessee also witnessed the carnage on the slopes of Horseshoe Ridge. He wrote: *"I rambled about a good deal over the field where we were, and the havoc was frightful. The woods were full of branches and tops of trees, like a heavy storm had just passed through. Some trees more than a foot through were cut down by cannon balls. The underbrush was shorn off to the ground. One man was squatted by the side of a tree with his gun up, resting against it, cocked and aimed toward the log breastworks about fifty yards off. His head was leaning forward; he was shot through about the heart. He was a Confederate. Another was lying on his face with one hand grasping his gun just below the muzzle and the rammer in his other hand. Another lay on his back with both hands clinched in his long, black whiskers, all clotted with blood. He was shot in the mouth, and I think was a Federal lieutenant. About five feet off was another, his head gone. I came across a soldier leaning down over one that was dead, and as I approached him he was in the act of spreading a handkerchief over his face. He looked up at me and said, 'This is my captain, and a good one too. I want to send him home if I can.' I saw a good many looking over the dead for a comrade, and when identified would straighten him out, put a knapsack or chunk under his head, and lay a hat on his face; then perhaps cast their eyes up and around for some peculiar tree or cliff or hill by which to identify the spot in coming back."* (4)

That night Thomas was able to withdraw his corps up the road to Chattanooga and General Bragg's rebels were, themselves, too worn down and disorganized to mount an effective pursuit. In the end General Rosecrans was relieved of command of the Army of the Cumberland; Thomas took his place along with the name "Rock of Chickamauga."

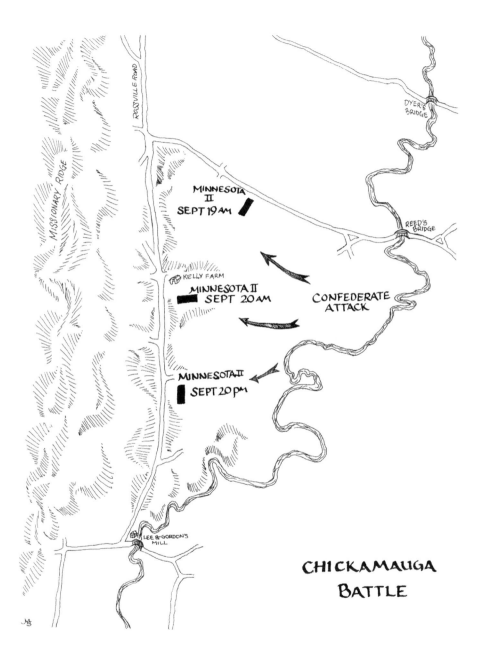

MISSIONARY RIDGE

ROSSVILLE ROAD

DYER'S BRIDGE

MINNESOTA II
SEPT 19 AM

REED'S BRIDGE

KELLY FARM

MINNESOTA II
SEPT 20 AM

CONFEDERATE
ATTACK

MINNESOTA II
SEPT 20 PM

LEE & GORDON'S
MILL

CHICKAMAUGA
BATTLE

Chapter 10
MISSIONARY RIDGE

Following the battle at Chickamauga the rebels had the Army of the Cumberland bottled up tight in Chattanooga. The southern lines extended for miles on three sides of the city and effectively cut off any simple route to resupply the federal troops. The only way to get food and materiel in was an 80 mile trek on a very narrow trail over the mountains. Because there was no forage available for the pack animals along the way, thousands of mules and horses starved to death making the round trip. They were joined by thousands more in the city. Over the coming weeks guards were posted to prevent soldiers from eating the corn meant for the artillery horses.

Rations for the union soldiers were cut in half and, a few days later, half again. They were down to getting two hardtack biscuits a day, a bite or two of meat, no salt or coffee and no fruit or vegetables. A plan was in the works to open a new supply line but would not be accomplished until after November.

The month of October marked the two year anniversary of Company C's departure from St Paul to the front in Kentucky. In that time the original 64 men had been whittled down to 42. The numbers were:

Discharged for Disability	8
Transferred	2
Killed In Action	2
Died of Disease	7
Resigned	1
Deserted	2
Total	22

Even with the army in a desperate situation, amusing incidents came up. William Bircher, the drummer boy, tells of one: *"On November 3 we four (I mean our squad) accomplished a feat which in after years seemed incredi-*

ble, and I know a great many will doubt it, but, nevertheless, it is a fact.

We were sitting in our tent and talking the matter over in regard to the scarcity of rations. As we debated the question, the conversation drifted to what we would have our mothers cook for us if we were home. After mentioning most everything our minds could think of, we had our appetites sharpened up to such a state that our mouths would water every time one of us would give a description of some dainty or toothsome viand. Finally, Jasper, the only one who had any money, offered to go down near the Tennessee River, where the division quartermaster was having some cattle slaughtered for the hospitals, and try to buy some meat.

I procured an order from the regimental surgeon, and, armed with that, Jasper proceeded to get the meat. In the short space of an hour, to our great joy, we espied Jasper at a distance coming with a large chunk of meat on his back, and were still more overjoyed when we found that he had succeeded in procuring twenty-four pounds, which cost him four dollars and eighty cents. We immediately got a large camp kettle and put in the entire piece, without salt, because we had none, covered it with water, and put it over the fire to boil; and the four of us sat around that kettle and watched until the meat was pronounced done. Now comes the story; we four, half-starved, half-famished men, drank all the broth from that beef and ate every morsel of the meat, without bread or anything as a side dish. I had an idea that some of us would get sick, but I lived over the night to write this in my diary for future reflection." [1]

With the near starvation and associated sickness, for both the federals and confederates, no real active fighting occurred. The skirmish lines were sometimes a hot place when, for example, a section of woods dividing them was cut down for firewood. On occasion the artillery of either side would, without any obvious reason, begin throwing a few shells toward the other. No men of Company C were hit, though several from other companies were wounded and one man killed from Company K. There was, however, another casualty in Company C; Christian Matti of Berne was medically discharged on October 12th followed by Charles Alden on the 27th for wounds they received at Chickamauga.

In early November the new supply route using the Tennessee River, known as the "Cracker Line" was opened and supplies began to flow like a flood thanks to the efforts of a Minnesota man. William LeDuc of Hastings was a Captain in the Quartermaster Corps and worked wonders finding and repairing steam engines and building small paddle wheelers that were used as supply ships. For his work LeDuc was promoted, eventually, to Brigadier General and made the Quartermaster of Sherman's army in Georgia.

By mid-November General Grant was in command of the army in Chattanooga, made up of Generals Thomas, Sherman and Hooker. The regiment was now commanded by Lieutenant Colonel Bishop, Colonel George having left for 60 days on a sick furlough. The stage was set for an advance against the rebels on Lookout Mountain and Missionary Ridge. The Second Minnesota was able to observe the action on Lookout Mountain, known as the "Battle in the Clouds" and then took a very active role as skirmishers out in front of their brigade for the assault on Missionary Ridge. The orders were to take the confederate entrenchments at the foot of the ridge and to hold there. This subjected them to tremendous fire from the rebels at the top of the higher ground. It became what is known as "a soldier's battle" where no single commander was in control. The men simply kept going up the hill, following the retreating rebels, using them as shields from the enemy fire. It was still a very dangerous situation; six of the seven non-commissioned officers in the color guard were killed or wounded. Colonel Bishop's report appears as an appendix to this book.

Chapter 11
WINTER 1863–64

To avoid the problems associated with three year enlistment terms expiring in the spring and summer of 1864 when the "campaign season" was in full swing the army took action in late December of 1863. It was announced that soldiers that "veteranized" would be granted a 30 day furlough, provided their regiment reenlisted a minimum of 80% of the men qualified. This required that each man sign up for another three years (or less if the war ended sooner). The Second Minnesota was one of the first in the Army of the Cumberland to fulfill the 80% and signed up enough men in only three days. A few of the companies did not meet the quota but the regiment, as a whole, qualified for the furlough.

Of the 27 men from Dodge County in Company C that were eligible, only 10 made the decision to reenlist for another three years. Those that decided to remain in the army only as long as their original commitment were temporarily assigned to the provost guard for the Division when the "veteranized" men were sent back home for a month. Those that reenlisted in the Second Minnesota Regiment of Veteran Volunteer Infantry were: Riley Barnhaus, William Bingham, Isaac Brelsford, William Casseday, Edmond Garrison, Amos Hostetler, Robert Hutchinson, Henry Lee, Charles Shedd and Morgan Wood.

These men departed from the front on January 8th on board two small steamers which took them to Bridgeport, Alabama, where a train picked them up and delivered them to Nashville. While in Nashville they were quartered in a vacant female seminary building which was warm and dry. The men were allowed to go about the city where, with a pocket full of just received pay, several found eating establishments full of the foods they missed so much.

William Bircher's diary entry for January 11th records: *"We received passes for the day to go into the city, where we saw thousands of soldiers on their way home on veteran furlough, and who, like us, were awaiting trans-*

portation. Among the novelties we saw here were the ladies, of which we had seen very few since our long and tiresome marches through the South. As they passed us on the streets, we were compelled to stop and gaze after them as if they were fairies." (1)

The ride on the train, in open boxcars, to Nashville had not been as pleasant as their stay in the city. One man, Charles Shedd, caught a severe chest cold and died in a Nashville hospital on January 17th after the rest of the regiment had departed to continue their trip to home. They traveled by rail from Nashville to La Crosse with several stops along the way. Arriving in La Crosse on January 22nd the men were loaded into covered sleighs and crossed the frozen Mississippi, arriving in Winona in time for breakfast on the 23rd. From there they traveled up the river by sleigh stopping at each river town along the way to accept the cheers of the residents. Their furloughs began on January 25th and each made his way home for his 30 days. The officers that accompanied them were put on recruiting duty, assisted in each town by any veteran that resided there. By the end of February when they gathered again at Fort Snelling their number included 150 new recruits.

March 8th found the men in Winona again, this time on their way back south. Edmond Garrison of Wasioja spent an extra day there because he, along with the rest of the Second Minnesota's band, had been invited to perform a concert for the citizens of Winona. They caught up to the remainder of the regiment at La Crosse and resumed their train trip back to the army in Nashville. From there they began a march back to the rest of the regiment in Georgia. Birchner's diary for April 5th: *"We marched to Stevenson, where we found General William Le Duc, of Hastings, Minnesota, who had charge of all the military stores there. He informed Mike Allen, of Company I, that, if he could get the consent of Colonel George, he would give the regiment a barrel of whiskey. The colonel gave his consent, with instructions that if a man should get drunk he would be severely punished. With these instructions, Allen returned to Le Duc, who at once had the head knocked out of a barrel and distributed the whiskey to the boys. Very few of them showed any signs of intoxication. After a short stay with General Le Duc, we continued our march, arriving at Chattanooga at 10:00 p.m. and were quartered in the Soldier's Home for the night."* (2)

Meeting up with those of the regiment who had not reenlisted, or were not eligible, ended the furlough. The Second Minnesota now numbered more than 450 men again. Around this time, the beginning of May, word was received that John Stuckey, the man captured during the Battle of Chickamauga, had died in Baltimore after having been exchanged as a prisoner of the Confederates. His death brought the total thus far to 14 with an additional 9 having been discharged for disability out of those who had signed on from Dodge County. Samuel Kline had transferred to the Veteran Reserve Corps on April 30th. The VRC was a unit composed of those wounded too badly for active duty but could still serve as guards at prison camps and other duties. The number of Dodge County men still active in Company C now stood at 38 including the few replacements that had joined since the original recruitment three years earlier. James George had reassumed command of the regiment, Clinton Cilley was temporarily assigned to staff of the Division, and two men (James Williams and Oscar Heath) had transferred to the regular U S Artillery.

Chapter 12
SUMMER 1864

The Campaign for Atlanta was about to begin; for the next 100 days there would be no quiet moments with the thunder of the cannon and the rattle of muskets. General Sherman's orders were clear; he was to go after Joe Johnston and the Army of Tennessee wherever it went. He was not to be focused on capturing territory, though capturing Atlanta would be a very good idea indeed. The Army of the Cumberland along with the other armies under Sherman's command was to hound the rebels relentlessly, never giving them a chance to catch their breath. It began at Resaca and was to continue through the entire summer of 1864.

All through the month of June the federals were at it. The Second rotated at the front lines along with the rest of the regiments. Three or four days of life close by the Confederates, then a week or so about a mile back from the fighting to rest and refit. The southern army had no ability to do the same; all of them were up front constantly. On the fifth of June, just before the rebels began another withdrawal, Joseph Orcutt of Concord was wounded and captured. He was to die that September at Andersonville Prison. Through the remainder of June close contact and skirmishing was the daily routine; eventually something had to give somewhere. Toward the end of the month Johnston was backed up against Kennesaw Mountain. His lines were formidable and the artillery were well sighted in. It was a time for Sherman to be careful, but the incessantly slow push was wearing on his patience. He determined to make one great push against the rebel lines and break them. It was at this time that Colonel Bishop speaks of: *"The enemy amused themselves two or three times a day by shelling our camps vigorously for a few minutes to see the 'Yanks' run for the breastworks. Here the muster out rolls were prepared and orders obtained for the discharge of our non-veterans, whose three-year term was nearly expired. Colonel George announced his intention to retire also at the end of his term and received orders on the twenty-*

second to go to Chattanooga on the twenty-third with the non-veterans, there to be mustered out. The colonel's age and physical infirmity disqualified him for a hard campaign like this, but he persisted to the completion of his term and left us at last much to our regret and his own.

About midnight on the twenty-second, our regiment was ordered to move about half a mile to the right to relieve another regiment there which was ordered elsewhere. It was a bright, still, moonlit night, and the enemy on the mountain was vigilant and in the habit of investigating with his artillery every suspicious movement, so the men were instructed to move quietly, keeping their gun barrels covered, all verbal orders and conversation to be omitted.

Our movement was thus safely made, but, on our arrival, the commander of the regiment to be relieved woke up his men at long range by shouting the regulation commands in a voice that could be easily heard by the enemy, who could also see the glimmer of their muskets in the moonlight, and, before his men were ready to move, a big round flash was seen on the mountain – a few seconds later, another, right in our faces, with a deafening explosion, and six men at the head of our regiment lay mangled on the earth. The going regiment took to the woods without any more formal orders, and our men took their places in the breastworks without any further casualties, though a furious cannonade was kept up for half an hour or more. One of the men killed was our Sergeant Major P.G. Wheeler, who a few hours later would have gone to the rear to be discharged. It seemed very sad that after three years' faithful service without injury, he should fall in the last hours of his term.

The next morning at daybreak, Colonel George and the one hundred and three non-veterans present with the regiment got ready to take leave of us, and with hearty good wishes and good-byes, we parted with them 'for three years or during the war.'" [1]

Peter Wheeler had enlisted from Dodge County, listing his residence as Sacramento. He left behind a wife and two children. His brother-in-law, James B Gere, had been killed in action nine months earlier at Chickamauga; his body was never identified and is buried in a mass grave at Chattanooga. Peter Wheeler is buried in Marietta, Georgia, in a national cemetery.

The summer brought more fighting as Sherman's army battered its way toward Atlanta. The city was a major transportation hub and manufacturing location, producing a vast majority of material required by the South. Capturing it would fracture the Confederacy into even smaller sections as the victory at Vicksburg had done the year before. Through the daily grind of fighting and marching and entrenching, men's thoughts often turned to that very important subject.....their stomachs. The drummer boy, William Bircher wrote of this:

"It is a question I have much debated with myself, while writing this diary, whether this chapter should not be entitled, 'hardtack,' as this article of diet was the grand staff of life to the boys in blue. It would seem that but little could be said of the culinary art in camp without involving some mention of hardtack at almost every turn. If you take a hardtack in your hand, you will find it somewhat heavier than an ordinary biscuit, but if you will reduce it to a fine powder you will find that it will absorb considerably more water than an equal weight of wheat flour; showing that in making hardtack the chief object in view was to stow away the greatest amount of nourishment in the smallest amount of space. I also observed that hardtack was very hard. This I attributed to its great age, for there was a common belief among the boys that our hardtack had been baked long before the beginning of the Christian era. This opinion was based upon the fact that the letters 'B.C.' were stamped on many, if not, indeed, all the cracker boxes. To be sure, there were some wiseacres who shook their heads and maintained that these mysterious letters were the initials of the name of some army contractor or inspector of supplies. But the belief was widespread and deep-seated that they were without a doubt intended to set forth the era in which our bread had been baked." (2)

According to Bircher, the boys of the Second Minnesota knew of at least fifteen different ways to cook hardtack. The most common, and easiest, was to soak part of the biscuit in your coffee; referred to as "dunking," this served a dual purpose. It softened the hardtack to make it more chewable and also forced any bugs, such as wheat weevils, out of the cracker. You then had the choice of skimming the bugs out of the coffee, or merely eating them as an additional source of protein.

William Bircher also described another favorite food among the soldiers. *"It was not so plastic an edible as the hardtack, nor susceptible of so wide a range of use, but the one great dish which might be made of it was so pre-eminently excellent that it threw 'Hell fired stew' and 'Hardtack pudding' quite into the shade. This was baked beans. No doubt bean soup is very good, as it is also very common. But, oh, baked beans! I had heard of the dish before, but never had remotely imagined what toothsome delights lurked in the recesses of a camp kettle of beans, baked after the orthodox, backwoods fashion, until one day Bill Hunter, of K Company, whose home was in the lumber regions, where the dish had no doubt been first invented, said to me,*

'Come around to our tent tomorrow morning; we're going to have baked beans for breakfast. If you will walk around to the lower end of our company tent street with me, I will show you how we bake beans up in the country I came from.'

It was about three o'clock in the afternoon, and the boys were already busy. They had an enormous camp kettle about two-thirds full of parboiled beans. Nearby they had dug a hole in the ground about three feet square and two deep, in and on top of which a great fire was to be made about dusk, so as to get the hole thoroughly heated and full of red hot coals by the time 'tattoo' sounded. Into this hole the camp kettle was then set, with several pounds of fat pork on top of the beans, and securely covered with an inverted mess pan. It was sunk into the red hot coals, by which it was completely concealed, and was left there all night to bake, one of the camp guards throwing a log on the fire from time to time to keep matters going.

Early the next morning someone shook me roughly as I lay sleeping soundly in my tent: 'Get up, Billy! Breakfast is ready. Come to our tent. If you never ate baked beans before, you never ate anything worth eating.'

I found three or four of the boys seated around the camp kettle, each with a tin plate on his knee and a spoon in his hand, doing his very best to establish the truth of the old adage, 'The proof of the pudding is in the eating.' Now, it is a far more difficult matter to describe the experiences of the palate than of either the eye or the ear, and, therefore, I shall not attempt to tell how very good baked beans are.

The only trouble with a camp kettle full of the delicious food was that it was gone too soon. Where did it get to, anyhow? It was something like Mike Dalton's quart of drink – an irrational quantity, because it was too much for one and too little for two.'" (3)

Chapter 13

FALL 1864

Atlanta fell to the federal troops after Sherman had cut all the railroads leading into the city from three sides. The final battle, Jonesboro, was fought by the 14th Corps on September 1st. The Second Minnesota, part of this corps, was assigned a position in the second line and, therefore, suffered only three wounded and none killed. Company C came through with two wounded, but neither was from Dodge County. That night Confederate General John Bell Hood, the new commander of the Army of Tennessee ordered the destruction of all military supplies and the withdrawal of the rebel troops. The noise of the ammunition dumps caused rejoicing in the federal lines; by now these soldiers knew the sounds of an enemy's retreat.

When Hood left the city he headed north in the hope of drawing Sherman away from Atlanta, stringing him out, allowing the rebels to cut the union supply lines. This was his plan; but not General Sherman's. The federal troops chased Hood for a few days but then allowed the confederates to continue on their way. Sherman had his own plan; the Army of the Cumberland under General Thomas was to handle Hood. The rest of Sherman's troops, more than 60,000 of them, would return to Atlanta and prepare for another operation. The common soldier had no idea what was coming next. Sherman convinced Grant that he could strike out with no supply lines behind him and head for the Atlantic coast, foraging off of the abundant crops and livestock Georgia was known to be providing to the entire Confederate army, including General Lee's up in Virginia. As Sherman put it, his plan was to "make Georgia howl" and hasten the end of the war.

General Sherman ordered all civilians out of Atlanta, giving each a choice of traveling north or south but no choice of staying. On November 11th the rail lines north out of the city were cut along with the telegraph lines. The 15th found the army topping off their provisions, each man carrying three day's rations and 100 rounds. Wagons contained only coffee, sugar, hardtack and ammunition. Other than essential equipment this was all the army took along. Before the war Sherman had been stationed in Georgia; he knew very well the agricultural potential of the area the army was to march through. Three columns, each containing 20,000 troops would march south, laying waste to everything of possible military value along a path more than 30 miles wide. As the army marched out of Atlanta on the morning of the 16th with flags flying and bands playing, the city was "all in flames." The fires had spread from the military targets, like the railroad repair shops, to the nearby houses. A large part of the city became ashes as the army left.

Years later, Colonel Bishop wrote of the March to the Sea as part of the official history of the war commissioned by the State of Minnesota. He wrote: *"Our course was eastward, parallel and near to the track of the Georgia Railroad; passing through Decatur, and near Stone Mountain, we encamped early after an easy march of fifteen miles. In the next day's march we passed through Lithonia and Conyers. We halted at noon for lunch and then our brigade wrecked two miles of railroad track before resuming the march. This unbuilding was thoroughly and rapidly done about as follows: Our regiment having stacked arms and unslung knapsacks near the road is formed in a single rank outside the track and facing inward. The rail joints at each end of the line being opened, the men all seize the rail with their hands and at the 'yo heave' command they all lift together, raising the rail gradually up and higher and finally overturning the entire track. The rails are joined only with the old-fashioned chairs, and in falling on its back the track is shaken up and loosened. The ties are now knocked off and piled upon the roadbed cob-house-wise, a few dry fence rails mixed in for kindling; the fire is started and the iron rails being laid across the pile are in a short time red hot at the center. A lever and hook is now put on each end of each rail and the ends are so turned in opposite directions and brought down to the ground as to give the rail at once a spiral twist and a 'Grecian bend' along its middle third. Sometimes the boys would give them an extra heating and wind them around the trees by the roadside, and at every mile-post the letters U.S. in sixty-pound rails were set up to encourage the loyalty of those who might see and read."* [1]

So it went, mile after mile and day after day. The army was laying waste to the rail lines, factories, storehouses, mills and anything else of military value to the Confederacy. Sherman was out to prove that the South was an empty shell; that the enemy had no means of stopping him or protecting the civilians in Georgia. His message to southern leaders was that only they could stop it, by surrendering and returning to the Union. As to obtaining food supplies the army needed, Colonel Bishop also wrote: *"We had been eight days on the road from Atlanta and thus far had drawn no rations from our wagons except coffee. There had been, however, no lack of provisions; it was in that country the season of plenty; there had been cultivated by the negro labor a most bountiful crop of corn, sweet potatoes and various vegetables, and on every plantation were fat cattle, pigs and poultry in abundance, while the smoke houses were filled with hams and bacon just cured. Butter, honey, sorghum syrup, apples, home-made jelly and preserves and pickles had been also provided and stored for us, and it wasn't necessary even to ask for them. Every morning an officer with a sergeant and ten men (one from each company) were sent out to provide a day's subsistence for the regiment. These details were called foragers or 'bummers.' They were of course armed and kept together and were thus able to whip, or at least stand off, any party of the enemy's cavalry they might meet. Details from other regiments that scattered and straggled lost a good many men by capture, but not a single man of ours was so lost, either from the foragers or the column, during the entire march to Savannah. These foragers would get as far ahead as they could in the first hour or two, then leave the road and visit the plantations, find a wagon or cart, or perhaps a carriage and a single or pair of horses, or mules, or oxen, or cows to haul it, load it with corn meal, potatoes, hams, poultry and everything else they could find that was edible, and, leading a fat steer or two, would return to the roadside and join in the column as the regiment came along. The quantity and quality of supplies thus collected by these foragers was more than sufficient, and the grotesque appearance of the bummers as they lined the roadside in the afternoon waiting to join their regiments was a never-failing source of amusement. They usually went out on foot, but returned mounted or in carriages in all styles, from a creaking, rickety cart with a single steer or mule in rope traces to a grand coupe with a blooded pair in silver-mounted harness."* (2)

On November 23rd the army approached the capital of Georgia. William Bircher records the event: *"Marched ten miles to Milledgeville, the capital of Georgia. A few days before our arrival at Milledgeville the State Legislature, then assembled at the capitol, had hurriedly absconded on hearing of Sherman's approach. The panic seemed to have spread to the citizens, and the trains out of Milledgeville were crowded to overflowing, and at the most extravagant prices. Private vehicles were pressed into service by the fugitives. Only a few of us entered the city. The magazines, arsenals, depots, factories, and storehouses containing property belonging to the Confederate government were burned, also some seventeen hundred bales of cotton.*

Private dwellings were respected, and no instance occurred of pillage or of insult to the people. General Sherman occupied the executive mansion of Governor Joseph E Brown, who had not waited to receive the compliments of his distinguished visitor but had removed his furniture, taking good care, the darkies say, to ship even his cabbage." (3)

The march continued; the men entered a more barren section of south-eastern Georgia, getting ever closer to Savannah, their destination. Bishop wrote: *"Now we had left behind us the fine agricultural country of central Georgia, abounding in corn, hogs, cattle and sweet potatoes, had also passed through a level section of sandy pine lands, almost destitute of population, improvements or provisions and found ourselves among the rice plantations of the Savannah River and coast region. The rice crop had been harvested, and the threshing and hulling mills were in operation. These were fired by the enemy at our approach, but our cavalry saved one of the threshing mills in the vicinity of our division, the hulling machinery being destroyed. So, for six or seven days, we had rice in abundance, issued to the troops 'with the bark on'. We had rice for breakfast, rice for dinner, rice for supper, and rice the next day and the next. Rice for the soldiers, for the horses, for the negroes and mules, and for everybody. The boys exhausted their ingenuity in contriving various ways of hulling and cooking it, but it was always rice, and we got so sick of it that some of us have never eaten any of the stuff since."* (4)

The regiment was within a day's march of Savannah when the news reached them that Confederate General William Hardee had ordered the rebels to withdraw from the city and march north into South Carolina. The Federals entered Savannah and marveled at the wide streets and tree lined avenues. The food available was better, too. In the waters between the city and sea were oyster beds which had not been harvested since the Union occupied Fort Pulaski and closed Savannah to shipping. The drummer boy, William Bircher, wrote in his journal for December 24th: *"Rather warmer. As rations were yet very scarce, we were informed that a short distance below Savannah were several large oyster beds. A detail of men and two teams went down to see if it was possible to procure enough for a Christmas dinner for the regiment. On their return we found they had succeeded in filling one wagon box; but they were of a very inferior quality. The natives called them the 'cluster oyster.' There were two to five in one bunch, and hard to get out. So our Christmas dinner did not consist of turkey with oyster filling and cranberry sauce."* (5)

When General Sherman took possession of the city he wired a telegraph to President Lincoln stating that he was pleased to *"present you as a Christmas gift the City of Savannah, with one hundred and fifty guns and plenty of ammunition, also about twenty-five thousand bales of cotton."* (6)

With the U. S. Navy in control of the waterways leading to the city it was only a matter of a few weeks before the Federals were re-equipped and ready, once again, to launch off on another campaign against the Confederates. There was a real sense that the corner had finally been turned; no one really believed there could be any other outcome to the war than Union victory. There was still the realization that the southern armies in the field had to be defeated; now, however, with the north's manufacturing and the great influx of available men to fight through immigration the die seemed cast. Even southern civilians sensed the end was near. William Bircher again wrote: *"Every other day we visited the city. One evening as a few of the boys were returning from the theatre, I being among them, we passed a fine residence, where there were some ladies in the second-story window, singing, 'Bonnie blue Flag' and 'Maryland, My Maryland.' We stopped and listened a few moments. When they got through, we commenced and sung that grand old anthem, 'The Star Spangled Banner'.*

I don't think there ever was such a surprise in that house before. I don't think 'The Star Spangled Banner' ever sounded grander or sweeter than it did that night in the still, dark streets of Savannah, sung by the boys in blue. They raised the window and requested us to sing 'Red, White, and Blue,' and the ladies accompanied us. They thanked us, bid us goodnight, and invited us to come down some evening and repeat the program." (7)

Chapter 14
WINTER 1864–65

On January 20th the regiment departed from Savannah. A good part of Sherman's army had already marched their way into South Carolina in pursuit of the war's end. The plan was for Sherman to make his way through the Carolinas and link up with General Grant's army outside of Richmond, nearly 400 miles to the north. General Joe Johnston was once again in command of Confederate forces remaining in the path of the federals. His idea was to make a stand and fight if Sherman's forces became separated on the divergent paths they marched on.

As bad as the damage inflicted on Georgia appeared, it paled in comparison to what South Carolina could expect. The common soldier held great resentment against the first state to secede from the Union. They believed that the past years of hard living, marching, fighting, and dying deserved a terrible revenge. It was said that when the army crossed from Georgia into South Carolina, not even songbirds remained alive. Journals and diaries of the northern soldiers contain entries telling of the killing of field mice and other rodents just so there would not be anything left alive!

Bernt Olmanson of Company E recorded: *"We left Savannah January 20th. We went in the direction of Augusta, Georgia, until we came within twelve miles of the city. Then we went towards Columbia, SC, Winsboro, Chesterfield, Cheraw, and into North Carolina. South Carolina was burning for 27 days. Very few houses were spared. Our army took a strip about eighty-five miles wide through the state. The Rebel army was around us all the time, but could not do anything. They had to leave Augusta, Charleston and other places because we burned the railroad.*

The soldiers went into the houses and took all they wanted, such as food and clothes, silver and gold, and often set the house on fire. No commands were given. The soldiers did as they pleased. South Carolina got what was coming. I often thought it was entirely too hard. I saw old people hardly able to leave their house while it was burning, and I felt sorry for the women and children.

Our soldiers often went far away from the main army for food and other things without orders. Often they were taken by the Rebel cavalry. Daily we found soldiers of ours dead in the woods. Their throats had been cut, but none from Company E." (1)

The men of the Second Minnesota marched nearly every day, destroying crops, buildings, railroads, and practically everything else. Some said it was their way of welcoming the state back into the Union. Weeks later, when they had reached the North Carolina border, a sense of restraint returned to them. Once again they only destroyed what was of military value and took only what they needed to eat. Colonel Bishop's report of the march through the Carolinas is included in this book as Appendix 5.

From the time of Peter Wheeler's death in June of 1864, excepting Joseph Orcutt's at Andersonville in September, none of the men from Dodge County had died. But in February of 1865, just weeks before it all was to come to an end, Owen Loomis took sick and died while the regiment was in North Carolina. His family made arrangements for his body to be shipped back to his original home and he is buried in West Pawlett, Vermont. Loomis was the 17th and last man from Dodge County to die in Company C during the war.

The Carolinas Campaign ended in late March when the regiment arrived at Goldsboro, North Carolina. There they received new uniforms and their first mail since the 5th of February. The men spent that day cleaning their equipment, and themselves, and reading mail and papers from home. The next day the Second Minnesota was ordered to march at the head of the Army of Georgia to Springfield, about twelve miles, skirmishing with the rebels the whole way. They stopped at the Neuse River where the bridge crossing had been burned by the retreating enemy. The next morning they received the news of Robert E Lee's surrender of the Army of Northern Virginia to General Grant's Army of the Potomac. The cheering could be heard for miles; but Johnston's army still was ahead of them and seemed full of fight. The march continued the next day toward Raleigh, covering another twelve miles to Clayton. One more days' fighting and marching of fifteen miles brought them into Raleigh. A day's rest and they again moved, reaching Durham Station two days later.

The men remained at Durham Station for ten days, during which time the negotiations for the surrender of Johnston's army to General Sherman took place. The paroling of the surrendered Confederates was left to another division and the men returned to Raleigh. It was during this period that word was received of the assassination of President Lincoln. Guards were placed around the various army units to prevent anyone from taking retribution on the local inhabitants. Officers were careful to monitor the troops closely and to take immediate action against any forms of violence.

Chapter 15
SPRING/SUMMER 1865

The regiment was ordered to prepare for a march to Richmond and on to Washington on April 30th. They were expected to arrive in the former Confederate capital about the tenth of May which required a daily average march of 16 miles. Having to carry only their personal gear and a mere 10 rounds of ammunition each, this was not a problem for a regiment that had marched so far in the preceding four years. It was almost a picnic to the veterans; march half a day, encamp with no guards about, plenty of food and clean water and perfect weather. They reached Richmond two days early and were ordered to camp outside the city. At this time no one was allowed to visit the area; all the men had to remain in their camps.

Colonel Bishop wrote of the last few days of the men's march to the nation's capital: *"On the fourteenth, we marched twenty miles, encamping near Danielsville, and, on the fifteenth, after passing through Verdiersville, we crossed the Rapidan at Racoon Ford, nineteen miles. On the sixteenth, we made eighteen miles, crossing the Rappahannock at Kelly's Ford and next day marched eighteen miles and encamped at Bristoe Station on the Orange & Alexandria Railroad.*

We were now traversing historic ground and were much interested in noting places whose names were so familiar in association with the movements of the Army of the Potomac. On the eighteenth, we passed Manassas Junction, the Bull Run battlefield, and Centerville in a march of twenty miles and, on the nineteenth, moved our camp about six miles to Alexandria. Here, on the twentieth, seventy-two more recruits from Minnesota joined the regiment and were distributed to companies, and the commissaries, quartermasters, and paymasters supplied our needs in their respective departments.

Orders were received announcing the Grand Final Review in Washington of the two great representative armies, that of the Army of the Potomac on the twenty-third and of Sherman's Army on the twenty-fourth of May, and a day or two was given for rest and preparation. Our regiment was in splendid condition and well armed and equipped in every particular. We numbered about 300 veterans of nearly four years' service, and 400 recruits of one year or less, but these had been so well mingled with and instructed by the veterans that there was little apparent difference in appearance or efficiency." [1]

This celebration would be larger and more spectacular than the two days the capital had enjoyed between Lee's surrender and Lincoln's assassination. The first day highlighted the Army of the Potomac under General George Meade; these were the troops that had protected Washington for four years. Their march through the city, 12 men abreast, took more than eight hours. The cavalry alone marched in a formation more than seven miles long. All "spit and polish," Meade's soldiers looked and marched like the disciplined troops everyone expected. The next day was reserved for a review of Sherman's Armies of Georgia, Tennessee and the Cumberland.

When Sherman's men arrived in the capital a few days earlier, they were camped across the Potomac from Meade's army. Though this hindered direct contact between these two with their well known "sibling rivalry," the city's bars and brothels, coupled with ample opportunity for soldiers to visit, allowed for a multitude of fistfights to take place. Certainly the provost guard was kept busy on the eve of the parades.

The second day showcased an army like no other that had been seen during the war by the spectators. The weathered, tanned men had dressed up their uniforms the best they could, borrowing items from tent-mates and others. They marched as they had been taught long before, in formation with straight ranks and polished guns held high. Following each regiment was a collection of horses, mules, even milk cows pulling carts and wagons full of "forage" and plunder, even livestock, sheep and hogs, taken from the Georgia and Carolina farms. Alongside the columns walked the blacks, the former slaves, now free, that had followed the army all the way from Savannah and through the Carolinas to Washington. The procession passed the reviewing stand for more than six hours, watched by President Johnson, many generals and other dignitaries and the hundreds of thousands of people lining the parade route. One young boy of about six watched from a window above the street; years afterward Theodore Roosevelt would march in a similar, yet smaller, parade as one of the Rough Riders. A bit later he would become President like Andrew Johnson.

Bernt Olmanson was not a participant in the victory parade. He was part of the provost guard remaining at the Second's camp to protect it. It didn't prevent him from writing a letter home about the day: *"Sherman's army is marching through Washington today on review. I am a lone housekeeper in the empty countryside. In Washington they did not know that Sherman's army was anything. There were not enough clothes for more than one third of the army. Our pack mules with kitchen utensils and other necessary things on their backs are in the review, also oxen with knapsacks as on a march."* (2)

The next week the armies were virtually disbanded and the men were already being sent home. It was expensive to keep an army paid and supplied, and the government was quick to begin the process of cutting down on the costs. The Second Minnesota, which had fought longer than most of the regiments in the army was not to be among the first sent home. Because they had "veteranized" back in January of 1864, they were to replace other units whose original enlistments were almost finished.

June 6th marked a day that made the men of the Second Regiment proud; Colonel Judson Bishop, who had led them through the long absences of Colonel George and who replaced George as the official commander, was formally assigned to command a brigade. With the assignment came a single star on each shoulder. The long, hard work had paid off for the man from Chatfield; he was now Brigadier General Bishop.

A week later the brigade, including the Second, was ordered to move to Louisville, Kentucky. After three and a half years, they were to end up exactly where they had started their journey in the south. The men were loaded into open coal cars, complete with several inches of coal dust on the floors for the trip. The train had barely started when the rain began to fall. Throughout the night they traveled in the rain; at some point they kicked out some of the floorboards to drain the water. The entire brigade gathered at Louisville on the 20th of June and camped four miles south of the city on the Bardstown Pike.

It was not until the 10th of July that orders were cheerfully received to prepare the rolls for mustering the men out of the army. The next morning the Second Minnesota marched out of camp, leaving the tents standing, passed through Louisville and boarded a train for Chicago. Their trip continued and the men arrived at La Crosse, Wisconsin on the 14th, immediately boarding a steamer for St Paul. The boat stopped at Winona and the men paraded through the town for nearly an hour. The regiment arrived in St Paul the next morning and the city turned out to greet them home. A new governor, Stephen Miller, welcomed the men and they were treated to a huge meal prepared for them by the ladies of the capital. After dinner they marched to Fort Snelling where they were detained a few days awaiting final payment by the army. On July 19th General Bishop made a brief farewell address to the regiment and the next morning all the men were paid and given their individual discharges.

As Judson Bishop wrote: *"The men dispersed to their homes with a loyal pride in the record made by the regiment, with a warm and steadfast friendship for each other as comrades, and with the satisfaction that comes only from duty well performed."* [3]

These words were echoed by William Bircher: *"We were then disbanded and said the last 'good-bye' to our comrades in arms, the great majority of whom we would never, in all probability, see again. And a more hearty, rough-and-ready, affectionate good-bye there never was in all this wide world."* [4]

Bernt Olmanson offers a bit different farewell: *"I started out on foot for home at sundown and was home for twelve o'clock dinner the next day, about 18 hours. I learned to march, double-quick, when I marched with Sherman from Atlanta to the Sea."* [5]

Of a total of 68 men that joined Company C of the Second Minnesota Volunteer Infantry from Dodge County, these are the 12 that were discharged the last day from Fort Snelling:

Riley Barnhaus	Henry Beaman
William Bingham	Isaac Brelsford
Jason Burdick	William Casseday
Michael Dresbach	Edmond Garrison
Amos Hostetler	Robert Hutchinson
Henry Lee	Morgan Wood

The Blue and The Gray

By the flow of the inland river,
Whence the fleets of iron have fled,
Where the blades of the grave-grass quiver,
Asleep are the ranks of the dead:
Under the sod and the dew,
Waiting the judgment-day;
Under the one, the Blue,
Under the other, the Gray.

These in the robings of glory,
Those in the gloom of defeat,
All with the battle-blood gory,
In the dusk of eternity meet:
Under the sod and the dew,
Waiting the Judgment-day;
Under the laurel, the Blue,
Under the willow, the Gray.

From the silence of sorrowful hours
The desolate mourners go,
Lovingly laden with flowers
Alike for the friend and the foe:
Under the sod and the dew,
Waiting the judgment-day;
Under the roses, the Blue,
Under the lilies, the Gray.

So, with an equal splendor,
The morning sun-rays fall,
With a touch impartially tender,
On the blossoms blooming for all:
Under the sod and the dew,
Waiting the judgment-day;
Broidered with gold, the Blue,
Mellowed with gold, the Gray.

So, when the summer calleth,
On forest and field of grain,
With an equal murmur falleth
The cooling drip of the rain:
Under the sod and the dew,
Waiting the judgment-day:
Wet with the rain, the Blue,
Wet with the rain, the Gray

Sadly, but not with upbraiding,
The generous deed was done,
In the storm of the years that are fading
No braver battle was won:
Under the sod and the dew,
Waiting the judgment-day;
Under the blossoms, the Blue,
Under the garlands, the Gray.

No more shall the war cry sever,
Or the winding rivers be red;
They banish our anger forever
When they laurel the graves of our dead!
Under the sod and the dew,
Waiting the judgment-day
Love and tears for the Blue,
Tears and love for the Gray.

—Francis Miles Finch

Reprinted from <u>The Photographic History of the Civil War In Ten Volumes</u>,
copyright 1911, The Review of Reviews Co, New York, Vol 9, pg 270

NOTES

CHAPTER 1

1   Minnesota Seminary Brochure of January 1861

CHAPTER 3

1   As reported in the New York Times, November 24, 1861

2   Pendergast, Timothy, Pen Pictures from the Second Minnesota, Park Genealogical, 1998, p 11

CHAPTER 4

1   Bishop, Judson, The Story of a Regiment, North Star Press, 2000, p 74

2   Letter from James George to Rhoda George dated January 13, 1862

CHAPTER 5

1   Bishop, Judson, The Story of a Regiment , p 89

2   Bircher, William, A Drummer Boy's Diary, North Star Press, 1995, p 21

3   Letter from Rhoda George to Helen George dated April 15, 1862

4   Letter from Clinton Cilley to Helen George dated May 14, 1862

5   Letter from James George to Family dated May 16, 1862

6   Olmanson, Keith, Letters of Bernt Olmanson, 2008, p 26

CHAPTER 6

1   Bishop, Judson, The Story of a Regiment, p 92

2   Bircher, William, A Drummer Boy's Diary, p 24

3   Carley, Kenneth, Minnesota in the Civil War, Minnesota Historical Society Press, 2000, p 69

4   ibid

CHAPTER 7

1   Bishop, Judson, The Story of a Regiment, p 97

2   Olmanson, Keith, Letters of Bernt Olmanson, p 42

CHAPTER 8

1   Olmanson, Keith, Letters of Bernt Olmanson, p 45
2   Bircher, William, A Drummer Boy's Diary, p 36
3   Bishop, Judson, The Story of a Regiment, p 108
4   ibid

CHAPTER 9

1   Cozzens, Peter, This Terrible Sound, University of Illinois Press, 1992, p 452
2   ibid
3   Bishop, Judson, Van Derveer's Brigade at Chickamauga, p 68-69
4   Lindsley, John, The Military Annals of Tennessee, Confederate, Nashville, 1882

CHAPTER 10

1   Bircher, William, A Drummer Boy's Diary, p 51

CHAPTER 11

1   ibid
2   ibid

CHAPTER 12

1   Bishop, Judson, The Story of a Regiment, p 155
2   Bircher, William, A Drummer Boy's Diary, p79
3   ibid

CHAPTER 13

1   Minnesota in the Civil and Indian Wars, Vol I, Pioneer Press Company, 1890, p 112
2   ibid, pg 164
3   Bircher, William, A Drummer Boy's Diary, p 91
4   Bishop, Judson, The Story of a Regiment, p 167
5   Bircher, William, A Drummer Boy's Diary, p 98
6   Brainyquote.com
7   Bircher, William, A Drummer Boy's Diary, p 104

CHAPTER 14

1   Olmanson, Keith, Letters of Bernt Olmanson, p 98

Chapter 15

1   Bishop, Judson, The Story of a Regiment, p 198

2   Olmanson, Keith, Letters of Bernt Olmanson, p 103

3   Bishop, Judson, The Story of a Regiment, p 202

4   Bircher, William, A Drummer Boy's Diary, p 127

5   Olmanson, Keith, Letters of Bernt Olmanson, p 106

CHARLES ALDEN

Birth: 1843
Death: 1928 • Dodge Center, Minnesota

Charles Alden enlisted in Company C on October 26, 1861. He was discharged for wounds received at the Battle of Chickamauga on October 27, 1863. He is buried in Riverside Cemetery in Dodge Center, Minnesota.

HEZEKIAH BAYLISS

Birth: June 18, 1843 • Madison County, Indiana
Death: January 28, 1904 • Concord, Minnesota

Hezekiah Bayliss enlisted in Company C on June 29, 1861 from Concord at the age of 18. He served his term of enlistment and was discharged on June 28, 1864. Bayliss later enlisted in the First Regiment of Heavy Artillery where he was commissioned as a Second Lieutenant. He was discharged from that unit on August 14, 1865. It is interesting that he chose to be remembered as a member of Company C of the Second on his headstone. He is buried in Concord, Minnesota.

CLARK BURDICK

Birth: December 3, 1842 • New York
Death: December 9, 1921 • Dodge Center, Minnesota

Clark Burdick enlisted in
Company C on June 29, 1861
from Mantorville. He served
his term of enlistment and
was discharged on June 28,
1864. Clark died on
December 9, 1921 and is
buried in Riverside Cemetery
in Dodge Center.

JASON BURDICK

Birth: New York
Death: Austin, Minnesota

Jason Burdick enlisted in Company C on August 21, 1862 from
Wasioja and attained the rank of Sergeant before being discharged
on July 11, 1865. He is buried at Oakwood Cemetery in Austin,
Minnesota.

JOHN CARTWRIGHT

Birth: 1840
Death: 1921 • Claremont, Minnesota

John Cartwright enlisted in Company C on June 29, 1861 from Wasioja. Cartwright was discharged at the end of his term on June 28, 1864. He returned to Claremont, Minnesota and took up farming. He is buried in the Claremont Street Cemetery.

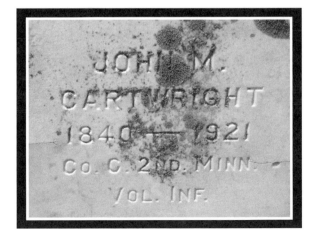

CLINTON CILLEY

Birth: February 16, 1837 • Rockingham County, NH
Death: May 9, 1900 • Catawba County, NC

Clinton Cilley was a teacher at the Seminary in Wasioja at the outbreak of the Civil War. Instrumental in recruiting several students along with his own enlistment, he was mustered in as

First Sergeant of Company C. He had obtained the rank of Captain by September of 1863. For actions during the battle of Chickamauga he was later awarded a Medal of Honor. By the end of the war he was a Colonel working with the

Freedmen's Bureau in North Carolina where he remained following the Confederate surrender. He later became a federal judge and was married to the daughter of a U S Congressman. He is buried in Catawba County in North Carolina.

MARQUIS DEVEREAUX

Birth: February 13, 1833 • Pennsylvania
Death: February 25, 1883 • Janesville, Minnesota

Marquis Devereaux enlisted on June 29, 1861 from Concord. He
rose in rank and was discharged as a Sergeant upon the completion
of his term on June 28, 1864. Devereaux was wounded at the
Battle of Chickamauga. He is buried in Janesville, Minnesota as
Marcus Devereaux.

AARON DOTY

Birth: March 1, 1825 • New York
Death: December 24, 1910 • Sauk Center, Minnesota

Aaron Doty enlisted in Company C on June 29, 1861 from
Concord at the age of 36. He served his term of enlistment
and was discharged on June 28, 1864. He is buried in
Sauk Center, Minnesota.

MICHAEL DRESBACH

Birth: December 2, 1836 • Mifflinsburgh, Pennsylvania
Death: July 20, 1918 • Dodge Center, Minnesota

Michael Dresbach enlisted in Company C on January 4, 1864. During his term of enlistment he rose to the rank of Corporal and was discharged on July 11, 1865.

After the war he was a leading citizen in the town of Dodge Center and served in the Minnesota State Legislature for a term beginning in 1877. He also served as justice of the peace and town clerk. He wrote a history of Dodge County and is often cited as a resource in Company C research. He is buried in Riverside Cemetery in Dodge Center, Minnesota.

JOHN FERN

Birth: 1839 • England
Death: April 19, 1884 • Kasson, Minnesota

John Fern's parents moved their family to the United States in
1843, first settling in New York. Both parents died when he was a
young boy of nine. He lived with various relatives and struck out
on his own, eventually settling in Dodge County in 1856. Fern
enlisted in Company C and served until he was wounded at
Chickamauga in September of 1863. He was discharged with a
disability on April 30, 1864 and returned to Minnesota. He is
buried in Kasson, Minnesota.

EDMOND GARRISON

Birth: May 16, 1836 • New York
Death: September 7, 1922 • Wasioja, Minnesota

Edmond Garrison enlisted in Company C on June 29, 1862 as a student from the Seminary and became a musician in the Second Minnesota band rising to the rank of Corporal before being discharged on July 11, 1865. He is the only Company C man buried at Wildwood Cemetery in Wasioja, Minnesota.

JAMES GEORGE

Birth: May 27, 1819 • New York
Death: March 7, 1882 • Rochester, Minnesota

James George was born in New York and married Rhoda Pierce in 1842. He was a veteran of the Mexican War settling first in Ohio following his military service. In 1854 he moved his family to Minnesota, obtaining land in Oronoco Township, part of Goodhue County. In 1858 George helped found the town of Wasioja in Dodge County. When the Civil War broke out in 1861 he helped raise volunteers for Company C of the Second Minnesota Volunteer Infantry. He was appointed Lieutenant Colonel of the Regiment upon its mustering into federal service. George became Colonel of the Second when Horatio Van Cleve was promoted to Brigadier General on May 16, 1862. George was in command during the Battle of Chickamauga, having returned from convalescent leave a few days prior. Due to poor health he resigned his commission June 29, 1864. He returned to Minnesota and practiced law in Rochester until his death in 1882.

PETER MANTOR

Birth: January 15, 1816 • Albany County, New York
Death: September 23, 1888 • Mantorville, Minnesota

Peter Mantor was the founder of the township and village of Mantorville. In 1854 he located a site for a saw mill on the Zumbro River. Mantor served as Notary Public for the new township and was in the state legislature in 1859 and 1860. He was commissioned as Captain

of Company C of the Second Minnesota on their mustering of June 29, 1861. While the company was in Fort Abercrombie, Dakota Territory in September his wife died. Mantor resigned his commission and returned to the business of operating his mills. He later remarried, for the third time; he outlived all of his children before his death in 1888. He is buried at Evergreen Cemetery in Mantorville, Minnesota.

CHRISTIAN MATTI

Birth: 1835 • Switzerland
Death: August 16, 1914 • Berne, Minnesota

Christian Matti was born in Switzerland. It is not known exactly
when he immigrated to Minnesota, but he enlisted in Company C
on October 12, 1861 along with another Berne resident, Jacob
Martig. Matti was wounded at the battle of Chickamauga, where
Martig was killed. Matti returned to his home at Berne following
the end of his enlistment term on October 12, 1863. He is buried
in the cemetery at Berne, Minnesota; Martig is buried in an
unknown grave at Chattanooga, Tennessee.

WILLIAM ORCUTT

Birth: March 17, 1840 • Ohio
Death: October 4, 1893 • Alma City, Minnesota

William Orcutt enlisted in Company C on June 29, 1861 from
Concord. He served his full term of enlistment and was discharged
on June 28, 1864. He is buried in Alton, Minnesota.

DARWIN ROSSITER

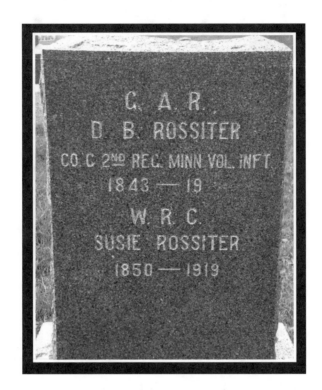

Birth: 1843
Death: 19   •   Dodge Center, Minnesota

Darwin Rossiter enlisted in Company C on June 29, 1861. He was
discharged for disability on May 16, 1862. Rossiter was one of the
students enlisted directly from the Seminary. He is buried in
Riverside Cemetery in Dodge Center, Minnesota.

MONROE WEATHERWAX

Birth: April 2, 1836 • New York, NY
Death: January 13, 1902 • Somerset, MI

Monroe Weatherwax was one of the original enlistees, signing up
on June 29, 1861. He was discharged for a medical disability on
October 22, 1862. There is no indication when he left Minnesota
but Monroe died in Michigan and is buried in Somerset.

COMPANY C — SECOND MINNESOTA VOLUNTEER INFANTRY

NAME	DISPOSITION	BURIED
ASHLAND (5)		
BEAMAN, HENRY	VETERANIZED, DISC 7/11/65	WOODBURN, OR
HEATH, OSCAR	TRANSFR TO 4TH US ARTILLERY 12/22/62	NEW PARIS, OH
HUTCHINSON, ROBERT	SGT, VETERANIZED, DISC 7/11/65	UNKNOWN
LOOMIS, OWEN	CORP, DIED 2/25/65 ROCKY POINT, NC	WEST PAWLET, VT
WHEELER, JULIUS	DIED 8/5/61 FT ABERCROMBIE, DT	CUSTER NATL CEMETERY
CLAREMONT (3)		
CARTWRIGHT, JOHN	SERVED TERM, DISC 6/28/64	CLAREMONT, MN
HARDIN, HENRY	DIED 2/21/62 SOMERSET, KY	CAMP NELSON NATL CEMETERY
OLINE, CHARLES	DIED 2/22/62 LEBANON, KY	LEBANON NATL CEMETERY
CONCORD (10)		
BAYLESS, FRANK	DISC 5/6/62 FOR DISABILITY	BOARDMAN, IA
BAYLISS, HEZEKIAH	SERVED TERM, DISC 6/28/64	CONCORD, MN
BONSON, URIAH	SERVED TERM, DISC 6/28/64	YORK, NE
BROWN, ALEXANDER	DIED 11/24/61 LOUISVILLE, KY	CAVE HILL NATL CEMETERY
DEVEREAUX, MARQUIS	SGT, SERVED TERM, WIA CHICKAMAUGA, DISC 6/28/64	JANESVILLE, MN
DOTY, AARON	SERVED TERM, DISC 6/28/64	SAUK CENTER, MN

ORCUTT, JOSEPH	CORP, WIA/CAPT KENSW MT, DIED 9/10/64	ANDERSONVILLE, GA NATL CEMETERY
ORCUTT, WILLIAM	SERVED TERM, DISC 6/28/64	ALTON, MN
RUSS, JOSEPH	SERVED TERM, DISC 6/28/64	WADENA, MN
WRIGHT, GEORGE	SERVED TERM, DISC 6/28/64	UNKNOWN

MANTORVILLE (22)

ALDEN, CHARLES	WIA CHICKAMAUGA, DISC 10/27/63 FOR DISABILITY	DODGE CENTER, MN
BINGHAM, WILLIAM	VETERANIZED, WIA KENNESAW MTN, DISC 7/11/65	SHIRLAND, IL
BRELSFORD, ISAAC	SGT, VETERANIZED, DISC 7/11/65	UNKNOWN
BURRELL, SAMUEL	SGT, DISC 5/13/62 FOR DISABILITY	ARENDTSVILLE, PA
CASSEDAY, JOHN	SGT, WIA CHICKAMAUGA, SERVED TERM, DISC 10/25/64	ROCHESTER, MN
CASSEDAY, WILLIAM	SGT, VETERANIZED, DISC 7/11/65	UNKNOWN
CHASE, NATHAN	DIED 1/8/62 LEBANON, KY	UNKNOWN
FERN, JOHN	SERVED TERM, WIA CHICKAMAUGA DISC 6/28/64	KASSON, MN
GERE, JAMES	KILLED 9/19/63 CHICKAMAUGA	UNKNOWN IN CHATTANOOGA
GRABLE, DANIEL	CORP, KILLED 11/27/63 CHATTANOOGA, TN	CHATTANOOGA NATL CEMETERY
GUILD, FERDINAND	DIED 1/6/62 LOUISVILLE, KY	CAVE HILL NATL CEMETERY
MANTOR, PETER	CAPT, RESIGNED 12/04/61	MANTORVILLE, MN
MORSE, THOMAS	DESERTED 1/1/62	UNKNOWN
ORCUTT, EDWARD	DISC 5/18/62 FOR DISABILITY	UNKNOWN
ORCUTT, THEODORE	SGT, WIA CHICKAMAUGA, SERVED TERM, DISC 6/28/64	MINNEAPOLIS, MN

COMPANY C — SECOND MINNESOTA VOLUNTEER INFANTRY

NAME	DISPOSITION	BURIED
MANTORVILLE (continued)		
ROHAN, MICHAEL	CORP, WIA CHICKAMAUGA, DISC 6/28/64	UNKNOWN
SHEDD, CHARLES	VETERANIZED, DIED 1/17/64 NASHVILLE, TN	NASHVILLE NATL CEMETERY
STUCEY, JOHN	CAPTURED 9/19/63, DIED 4/4/64 POINT LOOKOUT, MD	LOUDON PARK NATL CEMETERY
WEATHERWAX, MONROE	DISC 10/20/62 FOR DISABILITY	HILLSDALE, MI
WHEELER, PETER	SGT MAJ, WIA CHICK., KILLED 6/23/64 KENNESAW MTN	MARIETTA NATL CEMETERY
WILLIAMS, JAMES	TRANSFR TO 4TH US ARTILLERY 12/22/62	LEAVENWORTH NATL CEMETERY
WOODWARD, CHARLES	CORP, DIED 12/8/63 CHATTANOOGA, TN	CHATTANOOGA NATL CEMETERY
MILTON (8)		
BARNHAUS, RILEY	VETERANIZED, WIA MISSIONARY RIDGE, DISC 7/11/65	UNKNOWN
BURKHARDT, JOHN	CORP, SERVED TERM, DISC 6/28/64	UNKNOWN
DE GRAVE, RINTZIUS	KILLED 11/25/63 CHATTANOOGA, TN	UNKNOWN
GREENWALD, PETER	SERVED TERM, DISC 10/11/64	SANTA ANA, CA
HOSTETLER, AMOS	CORP, VETERANIZED, DISC 7/11/65	UNKNOWN
MARK, CHRISTIAN	DESERTED 10/6/62 — LATER IN 3RD MN INF	LITTLE ROCK NATL CEMETERY
MARTIG, JACOB	KILLED 9/19/63 CHICKAMAUGA	UNKNOWN IN CHATTANOOGA
MATTI, CHRISTIAN	SERVED TERM, WIA CHICKAMAUGA, DISC 10/12/63	BERNE, MN

WASIOJA (20)

Name	Service	Location
BURDICK, CLARK	SERVED TERM, DISC 6/28/64	DODGE CENTER, MN
BURDICK, JASON	SGT, VETERANIZED, DISC 7/11/65	AUSTIN, MN
CASTLE, FREEMAN	SERVED TERM, DISC 6/28/64	UNKNOWN
CILLEY, CLINTON	CAPT, TRANSFR 9/12/64, MOH CHICKAMAUGA	HICKORY, NC
COUSE, HARRISON	1ST LT, TRANSFR 11/9/64	DOWAGIAC, MI
DIKE, CHARLES	DISC 10/2/62 FOR DISABILITY	UNKNOWN
DOIG, ALEXANDER	SGT, SERVED TERM DISC 6/28/64	WINONA, MN
DRESBACH, MICHAEL	CORP, SERVED TERM DISC 7/11/65	DODGE CENTER, MN
GARRISON, EDMOND	CORP, VETERANIZED, DISC 7/11/65 — MUSICIAN	WASIOJA, MN
GEORGE, JAMES	COL, RESIGNED 6/24/64	ROCHESTER, MN
KLINE, SAMUEL	WIA MISSIONARY RIDGE, TRANSFR TO VRC 4/30/64	Dodgeville, IA
LEE, HENRY	VETERANIZED, DISC 7/11/65	COLUMBIA FALLS, MT
RICE, LEWIS	DRAFTED, SERVED TERM DISC 6/11/65	UNKNOWN
ROSSITER, DARWIN	DISC 5/16/62 FOR DISABILITY	DODGE CENTER, MN
SANBORN, LEVI	DIED 7/19/61 FT ABERCROMBIE, DT	CUSTER NATL CEMETERY
TOOKE, DAVID	SERVED TERM, DISC 10/26/64	KEOKUK, IA
TOWNSEND, ERVIN	CORP, SERVED TERM DISC 6/28/64	UNKNOWN
WELCH, JONATHAN	SERVED TERM, DISC 6/28/64	UNKNOWN
WOOD, BENJAMIN	DISC 5/18/62 FOR DISABILITY	UNKNOWN
WOOD, MORGAN	VETERANIZED, DISC 7/11/65	CENTERVILLE-WITOKA, MN

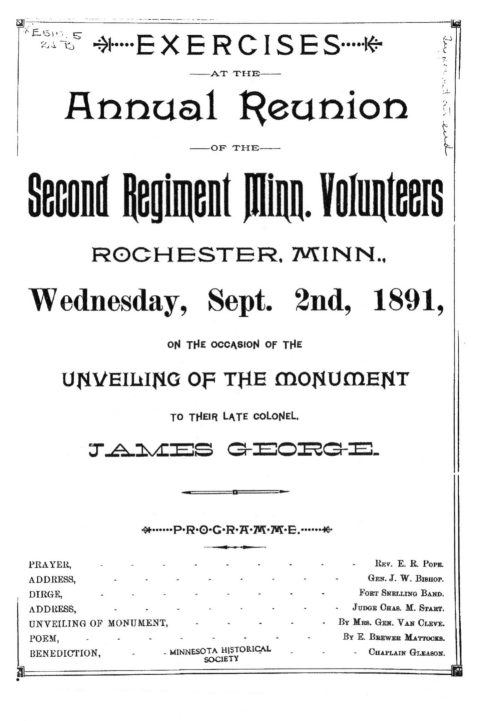

⇥···· EXERCISES ····⇤

—AT THE—

Annual Reunion

—OF THE—

Second Regiment Minn. Volunteers

ROCHESTER, MINN.,

Wednesday, Sept. 2nd, 1891,

ON THE OCCASION OF THE

UNVEILING OF THE MONUMENT

TO THEIR LATE COLONEL,

JAMES GEORGE.

⇥······P·R·O·G·R·A·M·M·E·······⇤

PRAYER,	Rev. E. R. Pope.
ADDRESS,	Gen. J. W. Bishop.
DIRGE,	Fort Snelling Band.
ADDRESS,	Judge Chas. M. Start.
UNVEILING OF MONUMENT,	By Mrs. Gen. Van Cleve.
POEM,	By E. Brewer Mattocks.
BENEDICTION,	Chaplain Gleason.

Comrades:

We have assembled here today to commemorate the life and services of an honored and prominent member and commander of the Second Minnesota Regiment.

More than thirty years have passed since he, with us, was mustered into the service at the Historic Post of Fort Snelling, and more than twenty-seven years since, upon the expiration of his enlistment, we parted with him under the frowning shadow of Kenesaw Mountain. Yet how well we all remember him. Noble and soldierly in form, voice and demeanor, he was a conspicuous figure in every assembly of men in military or in civil life.

We, his surviving comrades, are here to honor him as a soldier and to dedicate to his memory this monument, to which it has been our privilege to contribute. Standing here for all time to come, let it teach to all who look upon it a lesson of loyalty and conscientious devotion to duty. More than a quarter of a century now intervenes between this ceremony and the close of the war. A generation of young men, born since we were mustered out of the service, were old enough to vote at the presidential election three years ago. Let us hope that occasions like these will to them shorten the perspective, and bring into nearer view the terrible four years of war and sacrifice through which the blessings of peace and permanent prosperity that have come to them and to their posterity. And contemplating their cost, may they assume the active responsibilities of Governmental affairs with better appreciation of the precious trust committed to their hands.

As for us, old boys, unwelcome as the confession may be, we are reminded as we look into each other's faces, that we are growing old. In spite of rules and discipline we drop out of the ranks oftener and stay out longer, and here and there one lieth down to rise no more, while the column marches on. Van Cleve and Davis, and others within the past year have disappeared from our thinning ranks. Let us close up closer comrades, and keeping steadfastly in the line of duty, await the final summons, always at the "ready."

The address of General Bishop to his comrades had more of the paternal pathos in the appeal to them as of a father to his children than of their commander and everywhere, to the right or left, in front, tears silently stole down the bronzed veterans' faces.

HDQRS. 3D BRIGADE, 3D DIVISION, 14TH ARMY CORPS,
Chattanooga, Tennessee, September 25, 1863

Capt. Louis J. LAMBERT,
Assistant Adjutant-General, Third Division.

CAPTAIN: I have the honor to report the part taken by the Third Brigade in the action of the 19th and 20th instant, near the Chickamauga.

My command consisted of the Second Minnesota, Colonel George; the Ninth Ohio, Colonel Kammerling; the Thirty-fifth Ohio, Lieutenant-Colonel Boynton; the Eighty-seventh Indiana, Colonel Gleason; and Battery I, Fourth Artillery, First Lieut. F. G. Smith. Our effective strength on the morning of the 19th instant was 1,788 officers and men.

After a fatiguing march during the night of the 18th, and without any sleep or rest, while halting near Kelly's house, on the Rossville and La Fayette road, I received an order from Brigadier-General Brannan, commanding Third Division, to move with haste along the road to Reed's Bridge over the Chickamauga, take possession of a ford near that point, and hold it. I immediately moved northward to McDonald's house, and thence at right angles eastward toward the bridge. A short distance from McDonald's I formed the brigade in two lines, sent skirmishers to the front, and advanced cautiously, though without losing time, 1 miles. In the meantime brisk firing was progressing upon my right, understood to be maintained by the First and Second Brigades of this division.

Being without a guide and entirely unacquainted with the country, I am unable to state how near I went to Reed's Bridge, but perceiving from the firing upon my right that I was passing the enemy's flank, I wheeled the line in that direction and began feeling his position with my skirmishers.

About this time I received an order stating that the Second Brigade was gradually giving back, and that it was necessary I should at once make an attack. This we did with a will, the first line, composed of the Thirty-fifth Ohio on the right and the Second Minnesota on the left, moving down a gentle slope, leaving the Eighty-seventh Indiana in reserve on the crest of the hill. At this time the Ninth Ohio, which had charge of the ammunition train of the division, had not arrived. Smith's battery, composed of four 12-pounder Napoleons, was placed in position in the center and on the right of the line. The enemy having discovered our location, opened a furious fire of artillery and musketry, which was replied to promptly and apparently with considerable effect; for in half an hour the enemy slackened his fire, and his advance line was compelled to fall back. I took advantage of this moment to bring forward the Eighty-seventh Indiana, and by a passage of lines to the front carried them to the relief of the Thirty-fifth Ohio, which had already' suffered severely in the engagement. This movement was executed with as much coolness and accuracy as if on drill. Scarcely was the Eighty-seventh Indiana in line before fresh forces of the enemy were brought up in time to receive a terrible volley, which made his ranks stagger and held him for some time at bay. The Ninth Ohio, which I had previously sent for, arriving at this moment, I placed it on the right of my line. Still farther to the right a section of Church's battery and the Seventeenth Ohio, which had been ordered to report to me, were in position.

As the enemy slackened his fire, Colonel Kammerling, chafing like a wounded tiger that he had been behind at the opening, ordered his men to charge. Away they went, closely followed by the Eighty-seventh Indiana and the Seventeenth Ohio, the enemy falling back precipitately. The Ninth in this charge recaptured the guns of Guenther's battery, Fifth Artillery, and held them.

In the meantime the enemy, massing his forces, suddenly appeared upon my left and rear. He came forward, several lines deep, at a double-quick, and opened a brisk fire, but not before I had changed my front to receive him. My new line consisted of the Second Minnesota on the right, next one section of Smith's battery, commanded by Lieutenant Rodney, then the Eighty-seventh Indiana, flanked by Church's and the other section of Smith's battery, and on the extreme left the Thirty-fifth Ohio. The two extremities of the line formed an obtuse angle, the vertex on the left of the Eighty-seventh Indiana, and the opening toward the enemy. The Second Minnesota and the Eighty-seventh Indiana lay on the ground, and were apparently unobserved by the enemy, who moved upon the left of my lines, delivering and receiving a direct fire, Church opening with all his guns and Smith with one section. He advanced rapidly, my left giving way slowly until his flank was brought opposite my right wing, when a murderous and enfilading fire was-poured into his ranks by the infantry, and by a section shotted with canister. Notwithstanding this he steadily moved up his second and third lines. Having observed his great force as well as the persistency of his attack, I had sent messenger after messenger to bring up the Ninth Ohio, which had not yet returned from its charge, made from my original right. At last, however, and when it seemed impossible for my brave men longer to withstand the impetuous advance of the enemy, the Ninth came gallantly up in time to take part in the final struggle, which resulted in his sullen withdrawal. In this last attack his loss must have been very severe. In addition to the heavy fire of the infantry, our guns were pouring double charges of canister in front and on his flank, at one time delivered at a distance not exceeding 40 yards. During the latter part of the contest re-enforcements had arrived, and were by General Brannan, then present, formed in line for the purpose of supporting my brigade, but they were not actively engaged at this time.

Our dead and wounded were gathered up, and a new line, under the supervision of General Brannan, was formed. The enemy, however, made no further demonstration, and quietly withdrew. A small number of prisoners were taken, who reported that the force opposed to us was two divisions of Longstreet's corps, one commanded by General Hood. They fought with great obstinacy and determination, only retreating when fairly swept away by our overwhelming fire.

After the second withdrawal of the enemy, our empty cartridge-boxes were replenished from wagons sent on the field by the general commanding division. After resting my command for an hour or more, I was ordered to report to Major-General Reynolds. Immediately moving toward his position, we arrived near Kelly's house just before sundown, and there, by direction of General Brannan, went into bivouac.

At 8 o'clock the next morning, Sunday, the 20th September, 1863, my brigade was posted as a reserve in rear of the First and Second Brigades of the division, formed in two lines of columns closed en masse, where we remained for about an hour, slowly moving over toward the left for the purpose of occupying the space between the Third and Reynolds' divisions. Here I received an order to move quickly over to the left and support General Baird, who, it was said, was being hard pressed by the enemy.

I wheeled my battalions to the left, deployed both lines, and moved through the woods parallel to the Chattanooga road, gradually swinging round my left until when, in rear of Reynolds' position, I struck the road perpendicularly at a point just north of Kelly's house, near and back of his lines.

On approaching the road, riding in advance of the brigade, my attention was called to a large force of the enemy moving southward in four lines, just then emerging from the woods at a run, evidently intending to attack Reynolds and Baird, who were both hotly engaged, in the rear, and apparently unseen by these officers. I immediately wheeled my lines to the left, facing the approaching force, and ordered them to lie down. This movement was not executed until we received a galling fire delivered from a distance of 200 yards. At the same time a rebel battery, placed in the road about 500 or 600 yards in our front, opened upon us with two guns. My command continued to lie down until the enemy approached within 75 yards, when the whole arose to their feet, and the front line, composed of the Second Minnesota and the Eighty-seventh Indiana, delivered a murderous fire almost in their faces, and the Thirty-fifth and Ninth Ohio, passing lines quickly to the front, the whole brigade charged and drove the enemy at full run over the open ground for over a quarter of a mile, and several hundred yards into the woods, my men keeping in good order and delivering their fire as they advanced. The rebels fled hastily to cover, leaving the ground strewn with their dead and wounded. We took position in the woods, and maintained a determined combat for more than an hour. At this time I greatly needed my battery, which had been taken from the brigade early in the day by command of Major-General Negley.

Finding a force moving on my right to support us, and the enemy being almost silenced, I ordered a return to the open ground south of the woods; this movement was executed by passing lines to the rear, each line firing as it retired.

I learned from prisoners that the force we fought and put to flight this day was the division of the rebel General Breckinridge. That we punished them severely was proven by their many dead and wounded, among the former of which were several field officers, and among the latter one general officer of high rank.

I thence moved to a position on the road by the house near General Reynolds' center, and there remained resting my men and caring for my wounded for an hour or more. Although I had not reported to either General Reynolds or Baird, as ordered in the morning, I believe I rendered them very substantial assistance, and at a time when it was greatly needed.

About 2 o'clock, hearing heavy firing on the right of the line, and learning that the high ground in that direction was being held by General Brannan with a part of our division, I moved cautiously through the woods, and at 2.30 p.m. reported my brigade to him for duty. We were immediately placed in the front, relieving his troops, then almost exhausted. The position was well selected and one capable of being defended against a heavy force, the line being the crest of a hill, for the possession of which the enemy made desperate and renewed efforts.

From this time until dark we were hotly engaged. The ammunition failing, and no supply at hand, except a small quantity furnished by Maj. Gen. Gordon Granger, our men gathered their cartridges from the boxes of the dead, wounded, and prisoners, and finally fixed bayonets, determined to hold the position.

Here again the Ninth Ohio made a gallant charge down the hill into the midst of the enemy, scattering them like chaff, and then returning to their position on the hill.

For an hour and a half before dark the attack was one of unexampled fury, line after line of fresh troops being hurled against our position with a heroism and persistency which almost dignified their cause. At length night ended the struggle, and the enemy, having suffered a terrible loss, retired from our immediate front. During the latter part of the day the position directly on our right had been held by the division of Brigadier-General Steedman, but which early in the evening had been withdrawn without our knowledge, thus leaving our flank exposed. From the silence at that point Brigadier-General Brannan suspected all might not be right, and ordered me to place the Thirty-fifth Ohio across that flank to prevent a surprise. This had scarcely been done before a rebel force appeared in the gloom directly in their front. A mounted officer rode to within a few paces of the Thirty-fifth Ohio and asked, "What regiment is that?" To this some one replied, "The Thirty-fifth Ohio." The of-ricer turned suddenly and attempted to run away, but our regiment delivered a volley that brought horse and rider to the ground and put the force to flight. Prisoners said this officer was the rebel General Gregg.

At 7:00 p.m. an order came from Major-General Thomas that the forces under General Brannan should move quietly to Rossville. This was carried into execution under the direction of Captain Cilley, of my staff, in excellent order.

During the whole of the two days' fighting my brigade kept well together, at all times obeying orders promptly and moving with almost as much regularity and precision as if upon drill. They were subjected to a very severe test on the 19th, when, being actively engaged with the enemy, another brigade (not of this division) ran panic-stricken through and over us, some of the officers of which shouted to our men to retreat or they certainly would be overwhelmed, but not a man left the ranks, and the approaching enemy found before him a wall of steel. Private Savage, of Smith's battery, struck one of the retreating officers with his sponge and damned him for running against his gun.

Our loss in the engagements of both days amounts to 13 officers and 132 men killed, and 25 officers and 581 men wounded, and 5l missing, the total loss being 802 men and officers.

Doubtless many of those enumerated among the missing will be found either wounded or killed. There was no straggling, and I have little doubt those not wounded or killed will be found prisoners in the hands of the enemy.

It is a noticeable fact that the Second Minnesota had not a single man among the missing or a straggler during the two days' engagement.

I cannot speak too highly of the conduct of my officers and men. Without exception they performed all that was required, much more than should have been expected. Where all did so well it seems almost unjust to make distinctions. More gallantry and indomitable courage was never displayed upon the field of battle.

The attention of the general commanding the division is particularly called to the conduct of Col. James George, Second Minnesota; Col. Gustave Kammerling, Ninth Ohio; Col. N. Gleason, Eighty-seventh Indiana; Lieut. Col. H. V. N. Boynton, commanding Thirty-fifth Ohio; and First Lieut. Frank Guest Smith, commanding Battery I, Fourth Artillery. These officers performed every duty required of them with coolness and great promptness, and by their energy and gallantry contributed much to the favorable result which attended every collision with the enemy. Such officers are a credit to the service and our country.

Smith's battery rendered great help in the action of the l9th, and was ably and gallantly served, Lieutenant Rodney being conspicuous in the management of his section.

Captain Church, of the First Brigade, with one section of his battery, fought well and is entitled to credit for the assistance he rendered me on the 19th. I cannot refrain from alluding to the reckless courage and dash of Adjutant Harries, Ninth Ohio. My staff upon the field consisted of Capt. J. R. Beatty, of Second Minnesota, acting assistant adjutant-general; Capt. Oliver H. Parshall, of the Thirty fifth Ohio, and Capt. E. B. Thoenssen, Ninth Ohio, acting aides; Capt. C. A. Cilley, Second Minnesota, brigade topographical engineer; and First Lieut. A. E. Alden, brigade inspector. For efficiency, personal courage, and energy their conduct deserves more than praise. They exposed themselves upon all occasions, watching the movements of the enemy, carrying orders, rallying the men, and by every means in their power contributing to the success of the brigade. Captain Parshall was killed early in the action of the first day. He was a brave, noble soldier, an upright gentleman, and carries with him to the grave the love and regret of many friends. Captain Thoenssen was missing the evening of the second day, and I believe was captured. Captains Beatty and Cilley had each two horses shot under them. There are many names particularly commended for courage and good behavior, for which I respectfully refer to reports of regiments and the battery.

We have lost many gallant officers and men, a list of whom is herewith furnished you. In the charge made by the Ninth Ohio on the 19th, when they recaptured the battery of the regular brigade, their loss in killed and wounded was over 50.

I am, captain, very respectfully, your obedient servant,
FERDINAND VAN DERVEER,
Colonel, Commanding Third Brigade.

Report of Col. James George, Second Minnesota Infantry

Headquarters Second Regiment Minnesota Volunteers,
Chattanooga, Tennessee, September 25, 1863

General: I have the honor to transmit the following report of the part taken by the Second Regiment Minnesota Volunteers in the battle of the 19th and 20th instant, near Crawfish Spring, Ga.:

The regiment was placed in position at 10 a.m. on the 19th, on the extreme left of the brigade and next to Battery I, Fourth U.S. Artillery, facing the south.

A few minutes later the enemy approached in line in front to within about 300 yards and opened a heavy fire of musketry, which was returned with such effect as to repulse the attack in about ten minutes. Another similar attack was soon after made and met with a like repulse, the enemy falling back in disorder entirely out of sight. About half-past 10 o'clock sharp firing of musketry was suddenly opened at some distance on our left and front, which soon began to approach us. The cartridge boxes had been replenished, and the regiment was laid down in line to await its time, the men having been admonished to withhold their fire until the enemy should be within close range. There soon appeared, approaching in disorder from the left front, a line of our troops in full retreat and closely pursued by the enemy, who was cheering and firing furiously in their rear. It proved to be the regular brigade, the men of which passed over our line and were afterwards partially rallied in our rear and on our left.

As soon as these troops had passed us the further advance of the enemy was checked by a volley from our line. A sharp contest with musketry followed, which resulted in a few minutes in the complete repulse of the late exultant enemy, who fled from our front in confusion.

About 11 o'clock a large force was discovered advancing on us from the east and simultaneously from the north. Our front was immediately changed to the left to meet this attack, and after a few minutes' fighting, the enemy seeming to be moving around to the northward, our front was again changed to the left under a hot fire, so that the regiment faced the northeast, and again finally to face the north as the enemy massed his troops for an assault from that direction. The enemy charged desperately, and were finally and completely repulsed and routed after a brief but bloody contest. The fighting ended with us at about 11:30 am. Our loss was 8 killed and 41 wounded, including commissioned officers; none missing. The regiment commenced the battle with 384 officers and enlisted men.

On the 20th the regiment took place in the brigade with 295 officers and men, 40 men having been detached for picket duty the previous evening and not relieved when the regiment marched. At 10 a.m. the regiment on the right of the brigade was advanced into an open field to the support of a battery which was in action immediately on our right, the line facing the north [east]. Scarcely had the line been halted in its assigned place when a furious fire of musketry and artillery was opened on it from the edge of woods bordering the field on the west and 300 to 400 yards distant. The brigade front was instantly changed to the left, the movement being made in good order, though under fire; and our line at once opened on the enemy. After a few minutes' firing a charge was ordered, and we advanced at the double-quick across the field and into the woods, driving the enemy back upon their supports. Here the engagement was continued for fifteen or twenty minutes, when the enemy moved off by their right flank, clearing our front and getting out of our range, even when firing to the left oblique. The regiment was then withdrawn and the brigade re-formed, facing the south [north]. Presently an artillery fire was opened on us from the north [east] and our front was changed to face it. After remaining here in position for about half an hour we were moved off a distance of a mile or more to a hill on the right of our general line of battle, where, at 2:30 p.m., we again became hotly engaged with musketry. The enemy charged repeatedly and desperately on our position here, but were always repulsed by the cool and deadly fire of our rifles. The firing here continued without any intermission until 4:45 p.m., when the enemy temporarily withdrew from the contest. Two other attacks were afterward made on us here, but both were repulsed, and darkness ended the fight at about 6:30 p.m.

Our loss on this day was 27 killed and 72 wounded, being more than one-third of our entire number; none missing. Some eight or ten men of other commands, who joined us temporarily, were killed while bravely fighting in our ranks. I regret that AI cannot five their names and regiments. The conduct of the officers and men of my regiment was, on both days, uniformly gallant and soldier-like beyond praise. If any one of them failed in doing his whole duty I do not know it.

Asst. Surg. Otis Ayer and Hospital Steward Frederick A. Buckingham were captured from the field hospital September 20, and are prisoners in the hands of the enemy. A good portion of our wounded were left lying on the field and are now prisoners in hands of the enemy.

I am, general, very respectfully, your most obedient servant,

James George,
Commanding Second Minnesota Volunteers

Brig. Gen. Lorenzo Thomas,
Adjutant General, U.S. Army, Washington, D.C.

CASUALTIES OF DODGE COUNTY MEN OF COMPANY C, SECOND REGIMENT AT CHICKAMAUGA

KILLED

Private J Gere – shot through both knees (body not recovered)
Private Martig – killed first day (body not recovered)

WOUNDED

Sergeant M Devereaux – slight, in shoulder
Corporal J Casseday – slight, in hip
Corporal A Hochstetter – slight, in head
Corporal C Matti – severely, in leg
Corporal T Orcutt – slight, in leg
Private J Fern – slight, in arm
Private C Alden – slight, in leg
Private M Rowhan – slight, in foot

CAPTURED

Private J Stuckey – This man was detailed to care for the wounded men and was captured in performing that duty. He died in Baltimore, MD on April 4, 1864 after being exchanged and is buried at the Loudon Park National Cemetery.

MISSING

It is worthy of note (and included in the Brigade Commander's) that not one single Second Minnesota soldier was reported missing or unaccounted for after the two days of fighting at Chickamauga.

Headquarters 2nd Regt., Minn. Vols.
Chattanooga, Tennessee, November 30, 1863

Captain J. R. Beatty, A.A.A.G. 2nd Brigade, 3rd Division, 14th A.C.

Captain: In response to circular instructions of this date from brigade headquarters, I have the honor to submit the following report of the part taken by the 2nd Minnesota Infy. Vols. in the operations against the enemy during the week commencing November 23rd, 1863.

On Monday the 23rd inst. at 3:00 pm, the regiment marched from its encampment in Chattanooga with the other regiments comprising the 2nd brigade, with three days' rations and one hundred rounds of ammunition per man, and was placed in line of battle about half a mile distant from and in front or south of Fort Negley.

The regiment remained in position here until noon of Wednesday the 25th, when with the brigade it marched to the left, taking a position to the east of, and about a mile distant from, Fort Wood and facing the enemy's positions at the foot of and on the crest of Mission Ridge.

Here the regiment was advanced with two companies deployed, for the purpose of covering the brigade in its formation and movement towards the enemy's works.

The brigade being formed, a general advance was commenced at 3:00 pm and continued for a distance of about three-fourths of a mile without opposition, when the deployed companies reached the eastern or further edge of a strip of woods and came in full view of the enemy's works; the remaining companies being about 150 yards in rear of the deployed line and the remaining six regiments of the brigade about 300 yards still further back and partially concealed from the enemy's view by the woods in front of them.

Immediately in front of the deployed line lay an open field, the ground descending for a short distance to a small creek, and beyond it rising gradually for a distance of about a quarter of a mile to the crest of a low secondary ridge running parallel to, and about a quarter of a mile distant from, the foot of Mission Ridge. Along the crest of this secondary ridge was a breastwork of logs, occupied as the front line of the enemy's defenses by two regiments or battalions of infantry. Beyond it, the ground descended with an easy slope for a distance of three or four hundred yards to the foot of the main or Mission Ridge, which rises thence with a slope, gradual at first, but increasing in abruptness towards the top, to a height of five or six hundred feet. Along the crest of Mission Ridge were the main defenses of the enemy, consisting of a breastwork or logs, fully manned with infantry, and with artillery posted on the more commanding points in sections of two guns each at intervals of from one to two hundred yards.

The artillery thus placed swept with direct and crossfire the whole space between the ridges mentioned, and also the open field across which we had to advance upon the first breastwork.

In the valley between the main and secondary ridges were the enemy's encampments, the guns mostly hidden from our view by the small ridge and the breastworks in front of them.

The space between the ridges had been covered with woods, but, except the steepest and highest parts of the main ridge, where the smaller trees had been felled and "entangled" as an obstacle, the timber had been recently cut away and used in the construction of huts and breastworks.

After remaining in front of this part of the enemy's line for some twenty minutes, I received an order from Col. Van Derveer commanding the brigade to deploy my entire command and advance upon the first line of breastworks to seize and occupy it if possible; if repulsed to fall back on the brigade.

The men were briefly informed of the desperate service required of them and instructed to withhold their fire and to move steadily forward until the work was gained, and then defend it to the utmost.

The reserve companies were then deployed and, with bayonets fixed, the whole line commenced the advance. The enemy opened fire with musketry from the breastworks and artillery from the main ridge as soon as our line emerged from the woods, but in the face of both the men moved silently and steadily forward, across the creek and up the slope until within about one hundred paces of the breastwork, when, as the pace was quickened, the enemy broke from behind the work and ran in some confusion down the slope into and beyond their camps, where taking cover behind the stumps and among the huts they opened a brisk fire on us again as soon as we gained and occupied the breastwork.

Our line, now partially sheltered by the work, returned the fire with such effect as soon to drive the enemy out of the valley and up the slope of the main ridge, beyond the range of our rifles.

Our loss in the attack was severe, though probably much less than would have been suffered by troops advancing upon the work in regular order of battle. Fourteen prisoners were taken in this breastwork.

About twenty minutes after the capture of the first work, the brigade advanced from the woods, when the order was given for a general assault upon the enemy's defenses on the Mission Ridge.

My regiment moved forward with the others of the brigade, assembling on the colors as far as it was possible on the way, until in ascending the steepest part of the slope, where every man had to find or clear his own way through the entanglement, in the face of a terrible fire of musketry and artillery, the men of the different regiments of the brigade became generally intermingled, and, when the brigade finally crowned the enemy's works at the crest of the ridge, the regimental and even the company organizations had become completely merged in a crowd of gallant and enthusiastic men, who swarmed over the breastworks and charged the defenders with such promptness and vigor that the enemy broke and fled, leaving their artillery "in battery," and barely getting away a portion of the caissons and limbers. Six twelve-pounder Napoleon guns were thus captured by our brigade, two of them by the men of my regiment.

Hardly had a lodgment been gained in the works when the enemy's reserves made a furious counterattack upon our men, yet in confusion. This attack was promptly met by a charge en masse by the crowd, which, after a few minutes of desperate hand-to-hand fighting, cleared the ridge, leaving the place in our undisputed possession, with between two and three hundred prisoners captured in the melee.

The captured artillery was turned upon the retreating enemy and manned by volunteers from the different regiments, but darkness soon closed over the field and the firing ceased.

The regiments were assembled, and, after collecting and caring for the dead and wounded, we bivouacked for the night.

During the operations here recounted, about 150 men of my regiment, including two entire companies, "F" and "G," were on detached service, leaving but fifteen officers and 170 men, 185 in all, present for duty. Of these, one commissioned officer was killed and three wounded, and four enlisted men were killed, and thirty-one wounded; total of casualties, thirty-nine, or a fraction more than twenty-one percent of the number engaged. Three of the wounded have since died.

The ammunition expended averaged fifty-two rounds per man. Of seven non-commissioned officers in the color guard, all but one were killed or wounded, the color lance was cut off by a fragment of shell, and the field torn out of the colors by another.

A list of casualties is herewith transmitted.
I am, captain, very respectfully,
Your most obedient servant,
J.W. Bishop
Lieut. Col., Com'd'g 2nd Minn. Vols.

HEADQUARTERS SECOND MINNESOTA VOL. INFANTRY,
Goldsboro, North Carolina, March 28, 1865

Capt. S. FORTNER, Actg. Asst. Adjt. Gen., Second Brigade, Third Div., Fourteenth Army Corps,

CAPTAIN: In obedience to instructions just received from brigade headquarters, I have the honor to forward the following report of the part taken by my regiment in the recent campaign commencing at Savannah, Ga., on the 20th day of January, 1865, and terminating at this place on the 23d day of March, 1865.

On the evening of the 19th of January the regiment was relieved from guard duty in the city of Savannah and on the morning of the 20th rejoined the brigade and marched with it eight miles to Cherokee Hill, on the Augusta road, where it remained in camp until the morning of January 25th, when it marched for Sisters Ferry, on the Savannah river, passing through Springfield, Ga., and arriving on the 28th; distance marched, thirty-two miles. February 5th, crossed the Savannah river and marched up the left bank of the river for Barn well Court-House, passing through Robertsville and Brighton, and crossing the Salkehatchie river, and arriving on the afternoon of the 10th; distance marched, sixty miles. At Barnwell Court-House the regiment was detailed as provost guard and placed in charge of the town during the passage of the corps. February llth, at noon, the regiment was relieved and rejoining the brigade marched with it for the A. & C. R. R. near Aiken, arriving and assisting in the destruction of eight miles of the railroad track on the 12th; distance marched, thirty miles. February 13th, marched to Davis' Mill, on the South Edisto river, where it awaited the passage of the corps and trains; distance marched, ten miles. February 14th, marched at 11 A. M., crossing the river, and during the night arrived at and crossed the North Edisto river; distance marched, eighteen miles. February 15th, marched for Lexington Court-House, crossing Congaree creek at Clark's Mills, on the same day, and arriving at noon on the 16th; distance marched, twenty-four miles.

Marched the same day for Columbia and encamped six miles west of that place at Hart's Ferry, Saluda river; distance marched, six miles. February 17th, marched at noon northwards, crossing the Saluda river and arriving at Freshley's Ferry, on the Broad river, on the 18th; distance marched, sixteen miles. February 19th, crossed Broad river and marched up the left bank to Allston Junction, where the regiment assisted in destroying the railroad track, then turning northward and crossing Little river near Monticello, arriving at Winnsboro at noon on the 21st; distance marched, thirty miles. February 22d, marched northward along the railroad to Youngville, where the regiment again assisted in the destruction of railroad track, then turning eastward arrived at the Catawba or Wateree river, crossing near Rocky Mount on the 23d; distance marched, thirty-four miles. Here the regiment, with a portion of the corps, was detained for several days by a heavy and protracted rainstorm. The pontoon bridge was partially swept away by the freshet in the river and the roads and even the fields were rendered nearly impassable for troops or trains. February 27th, at sunset, the division commenced the crossing which consumed the entire night, and the utmost efforts of the troops in making roads and assisting the trains were required during the night and the whole of the next day to get the trains safely into park two miles from the bridge. February 29th, the march was resumed, though the roads were yet almost impassable and the weather bad, and on the 5th of March we arrived at the Great Pedee river crossing near Sneedsboro, on the line between North and South Carolina; distance marched, seventy-two miles. March 7th, crossed the Great Pedee at noon and marched for Fayette- ville, N. C., passing to the right of Rockingham, crossing Lumber river and several smaller streams, and with other regiments of the brigade occupied that town at noon on the 11th, driv- ing out the enemy's rearguard; distance marched, seventy miles. During the passage of the army my regiment, with others of the brigade, was on guard duty in the town. March 15th, marched towards Golds- boro, our division being in charge of the trains of the entire corps. The roads and the weather were very bad and our progress slow, until on the evening of the 19th we reached and crossed the Great Cohera creek. Cannon fire was heard in front during the day; distance marched, thirty-two miles. March 20th, the trains were consigned to the care of the Third Brigade and my regiment, with others of the First and Second brigades, marched on the Goldsboro road to the front, about six miles, arriving at 8 A. M. We were here until P. M., then moved into position confronting the enemy's lines [battle of Bentonville] with the appar- ent intention of attacking them. Here we were exposed at intervals during the afternoon to artillery fire from the enemy's batteries from which two casualties occurred in my regiment. At sunset we were moved back about one mile and encamped. March 21st, the [day] was spent in making and repairing roads, and on the 22d the march was resumed for Goldsboro, at which place we arrived on the 23d; distance marched, 38 miles. During the campaign the regiment has drawn from the trains one-third rations of hard bread, coffee and sugar; all other supplies have been foraged in the country along the line of march. A summary of the casualty list, hereto appended, gives: Died of disease, 1; wounded in action, 2; missing and supposed to have been captured while foraging, 5. Total, 8.

The total distance marched, not including foraging and work on roads or destruction of railroads, is 480 miles. The aggregate present of my regiment, when it marched from Savannah, on the 20th of January, was 526.

The decrease during the campaign of 63 days was: Sent to general field hospital, 11; missing, supposed to have been captured, 5; total decrease, being about 3 per cent, 16. Aggregate present on arrival at Goldsboro, March 23d, 510. "When I remember that about one-half of my men are recruits of but a few months' service, and that the campaign has been one of the severest on record, the very small percentage of loss in men missing and sent to the hospital during the march is more than satisfactory to me. I am equally grateful to the recruits (who have well outgrown that name) for their patient and determined endurance of privations and hardships to which they were unaccustomed, and to the veterans who have so uniformly given a soldierly example to those less experienced.

I am, very respectfully, your most obedient servant,
J. W. BISHOP, Lieutenant Colonel,
Commanding Second Minn. Vol. Infy.

List of Casualties in the Second Minnesota Infantry.

COMPANY B — Wounded in Action: Private William S. Lyman, March 20th.

COMPANY C — Missing, Supposed to be Captured: Privates Isaac A. Peterson, March 2nd; Sylvanns Stone, March 3rd; Mais Oleson, March 23rd.

COMPANY C — Died of Disease: Corp. Owen Loomis, Feb. 25, 1865.

COMPANY F—Missing, Supposed to be Captured: Privates Ferdinand Birck, Thos. H. Garreton, Feb. 12th.

COMPANY G — Wounded in Action: Sergt. Christian Sanders, March 20th.

MEDAL OF HONOR

During the American Civil War there were a total of 1196 Medals of Honor awarded to soldiers in the U S Army. Of these, 16 were awarded to soldiers serving in Minnesota regiments. A total of 10 out of the 16 were awarded to men serving in the Second Minnesota Infantry. One of these was earned by Captain Clinton Cilley, the former professor from the Wasioja Seminary. His Medal of Honor was awarded for bravery displayed during the Battle of Chickamauga while he was attached to the brigade staff. His citation reads: *"Seized the colors of a retreating regiment and let it into the thick of the attack."*

Another Medal of Honor was awarded to a Second Minnesota soldier for heroism shown during the same battle. Sergeant Axel Reed of Company K was under arrest at the start of the battle. To quote his citation: *"While in arrest at Chickamauga, GA, left his place in the rear and voluntarily went to the line of battle, secured a rifle, and fought gallantly during the 2-day battle; was released from arrest in recognition of his bravery."*

The remaining 8 Medals of Honor awarded to men of the Second Regiment were for a single action. Sixteen soldiers of Company H were escorting a supply train of wagons when they were attacked by 125 Confederate cavalrymen. This occurred in February of 1863 in Tennessee.

GENERAL STATISTICS
FOR THE SECOND MINNESOTA

	Regiment	DC Men in Company C
Date of mustering of first two regiments	June 26, 1861	June 29, 1861
Date of organization as a regiment	July 22, 1861	
Date of re-muster in as veterans	December 29, 1863	
Date of final payment and discharge	July 20, 1865	July 11, 1865
Number of men mustered into regiment	1735	68
Number of men commissioned as officers	91	3
Number of men wounded in action	274	21
Of whom were killed or mortally wounded	74	7
Number of men died of diseases	167	10
Number of men discharged for disability	277	9
Number transferred or promoted out of the regiment	76	5
Number reported as deserted	61	2
Number of officers resigned	40	2
Number of men discharged at end of three years' time	353	25
Number of men present at final discharge of regiment	699	12

While the regiment had various periods of encampment or post duty, it had also considerable exercise on foot. In 1862, 1863 and 1864 it marched, by the record, 5,153 miles, an average of four and three-fourths miles a day, including Sundays, for the whole time. No record was kept for 1861 or 1865. It is believed, however, that the average daily marching in those yeas would exceed that for the years given.

Copies of this book,
"The Boys of Wasioja"
may be obtained by contacting the author directly at:
michael.eckers@gmail.com

Contact the author to discuss volume discounts
for schools or fundraising opportunities
for non-profit organizations such as
local historical society projects
or American Civil War programs.

Michael Eckers has presented historical talks
covering the American Civil War
and the Dakota Conflict of 1862
publicly for more than a decade.
If you are part of a group interested
in hearing his presentation,
feel free to contact him
at the above e-mail address.
Speaking fees are flexible.